Playing with Things

The archaeology, anthropology and ethnography of human–object interactions in Atlantic Scotland

Graeme Wilson

ARCHAEOPRESS

ARCHAEOPRESS PUBLISHING LTD
Summertown Pavilion
18-24 Middle Way
Summertown
Oxford OX2 7LG

www.archaeopress.com

ISBN 978-1-78969-075-0
ISBN 978-1-78969-076-7 (e-Pdf)

This book is available direct from Archaeopress or from our website www.archaeopress.com

Contents

Acknowledgements v

Chapter 1 Introduction 1

A heuristic study 1

This study..2

The Study Area 3

The archaeology of play 5

What is Play? 5

Archaeology and Play..8

Themes and Results of this study 9

Bricolage 11

Placement 11

Extended Cognition 12

Agency and Play..13

Awkward Objects..13

Play and the world 14

Chapter 2 Playing Chess..15

Introduction 15

The rules of Chess..16

Some Chess Background 16

Chess and Cognition 17

Chess and Memory 18

Memory in Action...21

Thinking with things...24

Accounting for the Opponent..25

Materiality 27

Agency and Chess...27

Action by Proxy..29

Performing Chess...30

Chapter 3 Playing Euchre 32

Introduction 32

Euchre in its Context..32

Rules as Paths 34

Risk..34

Playing Euchre...35

The History and Rules of Euchre 36

Scoring at Euchre..37

Playing Euchre on Westray 37

The place of Euchre in Westray 40

The Players..40

How to win at Euchre 41

Following the Cards..42

Westray: A brief Introduction...43

Location		43
Economy		44
The Church		45
Risk Management		45
Farming on Westray		46
Rules for Farming		47
Selling Animals		47
Farming regulations		48
Farming with animals		49
Success and Failure/Bigger and Smaller on Westray		50
Back to the Euchre: Following not Leading		52
Cognition, Cards and Cows		53
Following Rules, Taking Directions.		55

Chapter 4 Counters **59**

Introduction		59
Sets		61
Bricolage		62
Art Bricolage		66
Found Objects		67
Shetland Counters		68

Chapter 5 Dice **74**

Introduction		74
Following Dice		75
Play and Ritual		76
Ritual and play		76
Parallelopiped Dice		78
Dating, Context, Condition		80
Dating		80
Context		81
Condition		82
Numbers		82
How the Dice Were Used		83
Rolling, throwing, placing		84
Atlantic Scotland during the Late Iron Age		85
Brochs		86
Wheelhouses		88
Souterrains		90
Broch, Wheelhouse, Souterrain		90
Changing Architecture		91
Changing Economies		92
Changing Artefacts		92
Some Reasons for Change		93
Discussion		94
Parallelopiped dice in their wider context		94
Parallelopiped dice in their local context		96
Dice, Play, Ritual		96

Chapter 6 Tafl **99**

Literary Sources 100

Tafl in Atlantic Scotland 101

From Notation to Action by Proxy 103

The archaeology of Tafl 107

Learning to play at Inchmarnock..107

Playing Tafl with Brochs 110

Buried Tafl...112

Chapter 7 Awkward Objects **117**

Awkward Objects 118

Awkward Type 1: Found Objects 120

Awkward Type 2: Surface Treatment: Painted Pebbles and Shetland Discs 123

Painted Pebbles...123

Shetland Discs...126

Awkward Type 3: The Wrong Context 128

Finally: some very awkward objects...130

Chapter 8 Final Discussion..**132**

Chess and Euchre 132

Archaeology and Play..134

Revisiting Huizinga 136

Playing with things..140

References **142**

Acknowledgements

This book is based on my PhD, which was carried out in the department of Anthropology at Aberdeen University and I would like to thank Tim Ingold, my supervisor, for his interest, help and *attention* without which I would never have gotten going, never mind finished. I would also like to acknowledge the good natured chess and euchre players in Edinburgh and Orkney, who never minded the odd question even if it interrupted the flow. The staff of Shetland museum provided access to the Clickhimin archive, unfettered and at short (30 mins) notice. I would also like to acknowledge Anne Brundle, now deceased and formerly of Tankerness House Museum, who one afternoon simply went around the cases with a tea tray, removing everything of interest so I could get a good look at it all. I would like to thank my examiners, Jo Vergunst and Richard Bradley who were both extremely kind and enthusiastic. Finally, I would like to thank Hazel for all her help, useful discussions, and forbearance. And Milos, for not minding.

I would like to thank Jenny Murray, Shetland Museum, for Figures 2, 5 and 8. I would also like to thank Alan Braby for his permission to reproduce his illustrations of the painted pebble from Bayanne in Yell, Shetland and of the Parallelopiped die from the Knowe of Skea, Westray, Orkney (Figures 4 and 6). All other illustrations are by the author.

Chapter 1

Introduction

A heuristic study

This book presents my encounters with play. It is a huge subject but my own particular interest lies with play as it exists in the archaeological record and was sparked by my encounters with play things during archaeological excavations. The material is interesting, and varied, yet I was frustrated by the available discussions since it seemed to me that they made no effort to get to grips with the subject. A typical archaeological site report might list the gaming pieces recovered, give their dimensions and describe the materials used, and then simply leave it at that. A good site report might include comparanda, discuss the date of the pieces and perhaps make a stab at identifying the game. I, however, wished to find out more about play generally, what it is and how and why people do it. I thought that if I did that then I would be able to look at the archaeological material with fresh eyes and perhaps reach a better understanding of how people lived at certain times, and places, in the past.

My approach has been taken from an anthropological direction because I felt that this discipline would have more to say about play, since it must be encountered routinely during anthropological fieldwork, and that it (anthropology) should have the theoretical depth by which it can be better understood.

Accordingly, as part of this study, I carried out fieldwork with modern people who play games. I gained a huge amount of information concerning play from this process, knowledge which is not available through archaeological techniques, and I then used these insights when I turned to my archaeological case studies. My study has also been reflexive, however; if I have applied my understanding of play to the archaeology, then the archaeology has also added something of its own to the whole; it has I hope contributed a unique twist to play studies.

I should also state here that the subject of this study is play and not the archaeology of play. I have explored the archaeology because it is what I know and because I knew beforehand that even if there are obvious lacunae in archaeological approaches to play there are also rich seams of material there. I go into more detail on the main themes of this book below, and as will become clear, these are not the things which one finds in typical site reports, or even in more general syntheses.

I call this a 'heuristic' study because I allowed myself to be led by my findings, rather than set out with a well-defined issue to explore, or problem to solve. I have not followed any overarching theme, other than the desire to find out more about play. I have simply followed those aspects which I found rewarding and insightful and these, as it turns out, are mostly cognitive; they are concerned with memory, the interaction between people and things, and the playful, or ludic, nature of life.

This study

When I began, I carried out a survey of the information available on the prehistory of Scotland, with the aim of gaining a general impression of the nature of the evidence for play, from the Mesolithic period onwards. The sources used comprised published excavation reports, in particular those in the Proceedings of the Society of Antiquaries of Scotland (PSAS), the journal of record from the beginnings of archaeological research in Scotland until the late 1990's. I have also consulted other publications such as the PSAS monographs (printed and online) together with various other site reports published elsewhere. As part of this, I visited museum collections in Orkney, Shetland and Edinburgh. I include my own fieldwork and experiences of excavation on various sites across Scotland, and make use of unpublished material from this fieldwork. I believe my survey to be thorough and representative.

One of the results of this survey was that I found it very difficult to identify any good evidence for play, in the form of board games, prior to early in the first millennium AD: one theme which emerged rather quickly concerns the problems with recognising the evidence for play in the archaeological record. I had no fixed criteria for this, however I was more interested in material culture, so did not pursue monumental structural features such as henges, or stone circles, or horned cairns, all of which could be interpreted in terms of performance and play, and I looked instead for the small objects which might once have been used as gaming pieces. It is difficult to define exactly what a gaming piece should look like, and I came across many contenders. Some artefacts are difficult to categorise and their purpose is ultimately unclear, for example, carved stone balls, or the carved stone objects from Neolithic sites such as Skara Brae, Pool or Quoyness in Orkney (figure 1). Some objects have also been treated in interesting ways which seem to make them stand out, for example by the application of decoration or their movement over long distances. David Clarke, Trevor Cowie and Andrew Foxon discussed many of these types of artefact (1985) and interpreted them in terms of power, prestige and display but their use probably also entailed ludic or play elements. The use of a carved stone ball, for example, may have required the adoption of roles for the participants. The ceremonies and situations in which it was used may have been more play-like than ritualistic. In the same vein, my review encountered many sites which could be just as easily interpreted in terms of play: henges and stone circles, for example, provide venues for performance; the areas delineated in front of the entrances to some tombs, such as horned cairns, would have set the participants in the ceremonies apart from the onlookers. Also, Chris Gosden (1994) has usefully discussed the way in which the form of temporality associated with these massive early monuments, such as Avebury, served to set them

Figure 1. Neolithic Carved Stone Ball from Links of Noltland, Westray, Orkney.

apart and it is *as useful*, I would argue, to view these monuments in terms of play as it is to interpret them in terms of ritual. I deal with the question of how to identify play in more detail in chapter 7 below.

The Study Area

When I began in earnest, then, my area of archaeological interest lay in a certain time and place: the Atlantic Iron Age of Scotland. The area includes the Northern and Western Isles together with parts of the Scottish mainland. The Iron Age in Scotland is usually taken to have a beginning around 800BC and continues to late in the 1 millennium AD, (Ritchie & Ritchie 1991) only coming to an end with the onset of Viking contacts from late in the 8 Century (Crawford 1987, Woolf 2007). I was aware that there was a large body of material which might be of interest and this particular material, as it turned out, was restricted more or less to the 1 millennium AD. In the event, I have stretched my Iron Age to include some material conventionally attributed to 'Viking' incomers, simply because it seemed too good to leave out. After this point, the picture becomes much more complex, not only in terms of the evidence for play but also as regards the types of evidence (literary references, in several different languages, become much more relevant) and the context – the large scale political and economic changes which are underway towards the end of the 1 millennium are by, say, AD1200, widespread and all encompassing: Iron Age Atlantic Scotland is no more.

The nature of the assemblages straight away pointed me in certain directions, and it was clear that most of the evidence derived from board games, as opposed to sport or physical contests. A consideration of play in the Roman world, for example, would naturally include structures such as amphitheatres, and sports like gladiatorial combat or funeral games, but this kind of site or activity seems to be lacking, or simply not visible in the Scottish Iron Age (though see chapter 6 for an alternative view).

With board games in mind, then, I turned to the anthropological side of my study and decided to begin with chess and chess players. I attended a chess club in Edinburgh and also one in mainland Orkney. These were both very interesting places and my strategy was simply to turn up and take part while paying close attention to how people played the game and how they interacted with each other. I had no underlying theories which I wished to explore, and I simply wanted to see what might turn up, but having said this I did have an interest in memory, as an active and skilful process, and was keen to see if chess might add something to my understanding. In the event, I believe that chess was a good place to start because it is a very clear example of this type of board game. The rules are not difficult and are entirely logical – one reason why it is frequently used by cognitive psychologists (Gobet et al 2004) in experimental settings. I found chess to be interesting and useful, however if there was a problem it was that chess players do not talk very much during play, preferring instead to concentrate and then (unfortunately) leave quickly at the end. This was particularly true in the Edinburgh Chess Club, where I spent most of my time. In Orkney the club was much more relaxed (meetings took place in a bar), however I still could see that there was a problem relating the game to its setting. I wanted to find out more about how a game and its players functioned as part of a small scale community, something which was difficult to appreciate in a city like Edinburgh where players came from very different backgrounds and places, and even in Orkney, since the players here came from all over the county to take part.

My solution was to step sideways and look at a card game, euchre, but this time the game took place on a small island in the Orkney, Westray. Here, I could examine how an extremely close-knit community played together and trace the connections between the play and life more generally on the island. I also had the advantage of living and working on Westray for many years as part of my job and thus knew many of the people who took part, as well as having a good general knowledge of how the island functioned, economically and socially. I was able to identify similarities between the play and life generally on the island, in terms of a kind of *following* (see chapter 3 below). I do not, however, mean to draw a tight comparison, or to say, for example, that since Westray is a certain kind of society that it must only plays certain kinds of games, or that there is an 'evolutionary' way of understanding the relationship – there is a theory that if societies develop through identifiable stages, for example from tribe or chiefdom through to industrialist state (Service 1962, 1975), then so should the games that people play: this is a common theme in some play studies, (see Sutton Smith 1997, 82-83 and Guttman 1994).

The other advantage of studying euchre is that, as a card game, it is a type of play which incorporates an element of chance – cards are dice-like in that the pack serves as a random generator, throwing up cards and combinations of cards in unpredictable ways. It therefore offered insights into games of chance, which was useful for my analysis of parallelopiped dice (a specific form of bone four sided dice, see Chapter 5 below).

The archaeology of play

When I moved on to a consideration of the archaeological evidence for play I faced some very real problems. The greatest of these is undoubtedly the question of how one identifies play in the archaeological record (see Chapter 7 below). This problem became more and more relevant because as I found out more about play I was slowly coming around to the belief that it is not always so set apart and I found many cases where the archaeology was ambiguous.

The boundaries between play and ritual, are acknowledged to be difficult to define (see Lévi-Strauss 1966, Turner 1969, Schechner 2002) but I found that the boundaries between play and 'real life' are also 'fuzzy'. Having said this, I could at least focus on a few cases which seemed, to me, to be definitely play oriented, which is how my archaeological case studies were arrived at: counters (chapter 4), parallelopiped dice (chapter 5), and Tafl (an ancient board game, somewhat like chess, see chapter 6). These three examples form the core of my archaeological study; they also, conveniently, span the 1 millennium AD and allowed me to consider something of the changes which occurred in Iron Age Atlantic Scotland during this period in tandem with changes in play; I said above that I do not follow a 'evolutionary' perspective yet if play is embedded in a given society then there will be links between the play and its setting which are interesting to explore.

What is Play?

What is meant by 'play'? On one level it seems to be a very obvious thing, an activity which is engaged in by all healthy adults and children. Some theories of play may make it appear simple, but it is in reality complex. It has the ability to morph, to change constantly and quickly, to start and finish suddenly. At its heart there is a sense of something which pretends to be that which it is not. Animal play is revealing. When a dog gives a play nip, it is both biting and not biting (Bateson 1972) – it is pretending to bite, and yet does this by biting. The other dog, or human, agrees that the bite is not real but pretend: a play bite.

We all play in different ways, however, so how do we know when play is taking place? How can it be recognised and distinguished from other perhaps more 'utilitarian' activities? It is clear that play is something which is predominantly active and in this sense it is a process rather than a product: play only seems to be present for as long as we are actually doing it, it leaves no residue unless one includes the tools for play.

It can also, however, be an attitude or a way of looking at the world and even very serious events can be made playful, or carried out in a playful manner. Play possesses an ability to infiltrate all aspects of life, which might make the thought of its study overwhelming and impossible, however it is for the most part well-defined: we know when we are playing and when we are not.

Historically, the study of play has been dominated by attempts to define its limits and to understand the subject through classification. Given the difficulties inherent in defining 'play' in a useful or practical sense, scholars have sought instead to establish subdivisions within it. One of the earliest modern attempts to classify play, and in the process to arrive at a definition, is that of Karl Groos (1901). His approach was based on a philosophical understanding of play as something 'instinctual', an impulse which is irrepressible and must find its expression through the action of play. He thus followed a 'Nietzschean' view of play as 'a kind of irrational power' (Sutton-Smith 1997, 112-113). Groos' classification is based on the body: he categorised play according to the sensations of touch, taste and so on. Play is also, for him, primarily a children's' activity, the impulse for which naturally lessens in the individual with increasing maturity. Play here arises as a form of experimentation or stretching of the body's senses towards 'real life' activity; there is no place for play once adulthood has been reached since there is no longer any need to rehearse actions which are now carried out for real. The obvious drawback to this approach is that it finds adult play problematic and must explain it as a 'hangover' or 'residue' from childhood or as an element of childishness in an otherwise mature life. This attitude, which is illustrated by Groos, remains influential and continues to inform present day attitudes to play as inherent within every person, and as naturally implicated in child development.

Johan Huizinga's study of play is undoubtedly the most influential of the 20 century. He followed Groos in as much as he saw play as 'primary' or an activity deriving from a biological or evolutionary need. For Huizinga, however, play was not pre-cultural but, rather, he asserted that 'culture arises in the form of play' (1955: 46). Huizinga did not classify *play* so much as he did *culture*, seeking to demonstrate the ways in which play is implicated in the history and formation of such cultural 'institutions' as language, war, poetry and art. Huizinga's major contribution is his definition, which can be summarised in three points (1955; 7-11):

- Play is always voluntary.
- It is well-defined in terms of both duration and location.
- Play is set apart from everyday life by the adoption of its own rules for behaviour.

A fourth point, equally important, is that play entails an uncertain outcome: without this, it drifts into the sphere of ritual (the 'favoured instance of a game', see Lévi-Strauss 1966).

For the theorists who followed Huizinga this definition has formed a foundation for most if not all further studies that is rarely, if ever, questioned. In addition, he also introduced 'Ludic' to the English language as a useful term for anything relating to play (see van Bremen 2002).

The concept of play as an activity which is always well-defined and set apart is the basis of Roger Caillois' (1962) classification of games into four main categories: Agon (competitive games, such as sports, chess, billiards), Alea (games of chance, such as betting, roulette), Mimicry (games of simulation, such as masks, disguises, theatres and 'spectacles in general') and Ilinx (games of vertigo, such as mountain climbing, skiing, horseback riding). It is with Caillois' definition that we arrive at a recognisable approximation of the basis of current play studies. Even if his categories group together types of play, such as sports and board games, which are now usually taken to be very different, it is the fact that the *qualities* of a type of play are being taken as the starting point for discussion which is important and one can see this approach where studies take those games which are considered to be similar and study them together as a group. Murray's corpus – board games other than chess - is one of the classic examples of this (1952). Here, he has grouped the games according to their qualities – chase games, war games, games of chance and so on.

If, as argued by Huizinga, play is seen as something set apart from everyday life, this makes the discussion of the relationship between play and other aspects of culture problematic. Clifford Geertz's account of cockfighting in Bali illustrates this well (1993). Geertz found cockfighting to be an essential, pervasive element of Balinese society but it is apparent, however, that since cockfighting is 'play', he treats it as having no intrinsic worth, or relevance; it exists in a kind of bubble. He insists, in fact, that 'The cockfight is 'really real' only to the cocks - it does not kill anyone, castrate anyone, reduce anyone to animal status, alter the hierarchical relations among people...' (1993: 443). His attempt to reconcile this contradiction led him to interpret the cockfight in terms of a *text*, the reading of which may shed light on society: '...a story they tell themselves about themselves...' (1993: 448). At the same time, however, he makes it clear that his, and his wife's, participation in cockfighting, as observers, led to their being accepted more fully by the Balinese and this point, I would argue, provides an illustration of how play, in the form of the cockfight, was not only formed by society but also that it was also actively implicated in the *formation of* society.

Caillois' (1962) study is one of the last to attempt an overarching study of play *per se*, as an entity. Mihail Spariosu discussed play in terms of rational versus pre-rational thought – he identified a schism in western concepts of play whereby it paradoxically occupies both positions (1989). In general, there has been a tendency for researchers to examine examples of play as it occurs in its setting either individually or as a class. Brian Sutton-Smith has, furthermore, identified a tendency for studies of play to be split along disciplinary or academic lines, such as between anthropology, sociology, psychology, education, child development and so on (1997). Sutton-Smith has also contributed his own list of play forms, which is slightly unusual in that his divisions are arranged in order from the mostly private to the mostly more public. His headings are: mind or subjective play; solitary play; playful behaviours; informal social play; vicarious audience play; performance play; celebrations and festivals; contests; risky or deep play. For Sutton-Smith, board games fall into 'contests' (Sutton-Smith 1997, 4-5), but it is clear that play is a vast, amorphous subject and that there is a great deal of debate over what, exactly, it really is.

Some types of play, including board games, have received relatively little attention, especially when compared to the ever burgeoning discipline of sports studies (see Loy & Kenyon 1969, Giulianotti 2004). Some areas of the world have attracted more attention than others from play scholars and it is difficult to say why this should be so other than a particular play form has caught the attention of passing anthropologists, perhaps because it has conveniently provided a contribution to some greater scheme of enquiry. One example might be Claude Lévi-Strauss and football (1966), or Trobriander Cricket (Weiner 1988). Japan currently seems to be a focus for attention in its own right (see papers in Hendry & Raveri 2002) and quite apart from the perceived oddness or otherwise of the Japanese at play, this may be due to a small number of anthropologists (Joy Hendry and Rupert Cox, for example) combining their own research interests in south east Asia with an interest in play, and in the process pulling in others to help develop the field further.

Archaeology and Play

There are many differences between archaeology and anthropology, even if they study essentially the same thing – people. For the purposes of this study I would characterise the difference in terms of movement: anthropology, for me, views things in motion, while archaeology is more static and must deal with the residue. Play, likewise, is a description of something in motion and here I have tried to bring some feeling for movement, or growth, back to the archaeology.

When it comes to archaeological literature generally there is little interest in play, unless it is part of wider discussions of childhood, or gender. Roberta Gilchrist, for example, firmly links miniature objects to children and to an engendering of individuals within society, though Joanna Derevenski is more cautious (Gilchrist 1999, 91, Derevenski 2000 and see also papers in Derevenski 2000a). The few exceptions are mostly confined to the classical world, or the Middle East. The 'Royal Game of Ur' (Becker 2007, Finkel 2007), for example, is an archaeological board game which has sparked imaginations. There is a small body of work on Mancala boards from North African sites (de Voogt 2012). Many Roman excavations have recovered gaming equipment; military installations in particular seem to yield large quantities of gaming material and there is a persistent trope of the lonely, bored, centurion whiling away his (it is always a 'he') long hours on watch by gambling or playing games with his companions.

In these accounts the games are always the unimportant activities which take place in between the real action, whether it be fighting off the natives or engaging in the far more important and worthy subsistence activities. Most archaeologists seem to (unconsciously) follow Groos or Nietzsche, I believe, in that the evidence for play is taken as the residue of childish, irrelevant activities. If there is one thing I hope to demonstrate in this study, however, it is the centrality of play to people's lives and how it can contribute to theories around the ways in which we interact with the world.

The closest that archaeologists' discussions come to *play*, with the sense of a subject which is bigger than mere *games* — Huizinga's 'ludic' — is probably when they deal with performance, or ritual. This is an interesting area, one where considerations of play, performance and ritual, archaeology and theatre, collide and intermingle (see Turner 1969, 1982 Schechner 2002, Pearson & Shanks 2001).

When archaeologists excavate a settlement they encounter the relations between the objects in a certain way — for example, even the best stratigraphic control cannot avoid a certain degree of foreshortening whereby numbers of objects which were used sequentially are recorded together as an assemblage (or bricolage); it is a problem I had to be wary of since it can lead to the accidental creation of sets (see chapter 4). The processes involved in museum storage and display creates more forms of this assemblage which can be difficult to disentangle; some museum displays actively encourage this kind of assemblage — the NMS prehistory displays in Chambers Street, Edinburgh are a very good example of this kind of foreshortened view because they deliberately juxtapose objects of widely different ages, in an attempt to present, for example, the evolution of pottery styles or the uses of worked bone.

Themes and Results of this study

> 'If it moves, salute it. If it doesn't move, pick it up. If you can't pick it up, paint it white' (Hutchins 1995, 7)

The results of this study fall into two main categories: those that relate more directly to the ostensible anthropological or archaeological subject matter of the study, and those which are more general. The general points are mostly cognitive and reflect my own interests to some extent; they revolve around the relationship between people and things, or objects. I noted above that I found chess players difficult to study because they talked so little, however they were in reality communicating a great deal, only they were using objects – the chess pieces - to do this. The same is true of euchre, and any board game. I was thus led by the anthropology towards a kind of cognitive study which took account of peoples' relationships with objects. The quote from Edwin Hutchins above sums up cognition quite well, I think. Hutchins is here restating a naval maxim but I like it because many of the problems identified by the theorists can be seen as revolving around these three entities: people, objects and the world. My study concerns all three, but it begins with the objects.

In archaeological terms, I was able to trace the first solid evidence for play in my study area from early in the 1 millennium AD onwards. This evidence begins with a limited repertoire of simple games using counters and gradually becomes more complex and more varied over time. By the end of the millennium, or soon after (Eales 2007), chess had arrived, in Europe at least, and is one of a group of board games such as merrels and alquerque (see Murray 1952, Hall 2007, Ritchie 2008) being played at all levels of society. One of the most interesting findings, for myself, has been how very widespread some of these games are. The earliest forms of game which I identified, counters and parallelopiped dice, most probably ultimately derive from contact with the Roman world much further to the south; these objects represent specific kinds of activity which should probably be included as part of the evidence for contact between Atlantic Scotland and 'Rome' together with the other more usual objects: amphora, coins, samian, metalwork etc. In the case of Tafl, the literary evidence demonstrates that it and its variants were played from the very north of Scandinavia southwards as far as Ireland, Wales and England. It even seems to have been incorporated as part of religious or cult activities (Page 1995, 206-207). The presence of this game in Atlantic Scotland is surely an indication of contact between here and Scandinavia at an early date, prior to the usually accepted (late 8 Century) date for Viking activity. It is an indication of the nature of these early contacts and must support Anna Ritchie's long-debated results from her excavations at Buckquoy (Ritchie 1977, Crawford 1987, 139-141), where she posited a degree of much more peaceful contact between native and 'Viking' than is sometimes assumed.

I have always enjoyed handling archaeological *things* — it is for me a definite plus when I am excavating on site and encounter an artefact — there is much that can be learned about an object when one can hold it and examine it in one's own hands; it is a process of discovery. It is not the same when I view objects on display in a museum, which are usually behind glass and cannot be touched and explored in the same way, but one of the pleasures of this study was the opportunity to look at objects which are held in museum stores. The Clickhimin material, for example, was held in a motley group of old tin boxes and cases which had not been opened for many years, probably since the excavation over fifty years previously. The objects have never been properly catalogued and so I never knew what exactly would come out next. It was this kind of interaction which brought home to me the importance of the object itself — its weight and size and also the material it is made of. I found that gaming pieces are made from a bewildering variety of materials: they can be made from animal bone, or pieces of reused pottery, some are shiny glass, others just waterworn pebbles. The most interesting ones for me were not the very fine or carefully made ones but the simple ones, for example the stones which had been plucked from the players' surrounding environment and pressed into service, perhaps only for the duration of one game, or cattle bones (phalanges) which had been modified only enough to allow them to stand upright.

Bricolage

It became clear to me that sets of gaming pieces are not always composed of identical pieces and that the process of play brought together objects which could be quite varied; this led me to a consideration of play, sets and bricolage (see chapters 4 and 6). I begin with Lévi-Strauss (1966), however he was concerned with a bricolage of the mind and thought (there are also many objections to his approach, see Ingold 2007), and my bricolage is of things, of objects. The juxtaposition of objects leads, I argue, to fresh ways of thinking, ways which cannot be entirely predicted before the objects are physically together, out there, in front of the player. I witnessed this process many times during games of chess. For a game which seems to be so cerebral, it is not always done in the head – players spend much of their time manipulating the pieces, moving one piece then taking it back and moving another. They do this to 'see how it looks' because even very good players find they cannot always understand a position fully if they cannot see the board in front of them, with the pieces in place. The exact location, or placement, of the pieces is therefore also important.

Placement

I found this to be true of chess and euchre but I also could trace this in the archaeology. In chapter 6 I looked at board games in the last part of the 1 millennium AD, and I did consider the placement of things in house interiors as ludic (there was also the attraction of the excavation technique of gridding the interior as a chess board), but there have been very few excavations in Atlantic Scotland which have recorded the data with the necessary detail and I would have been forced to take several steps backwards into the Neolithic before I could find the information — the ongoing excavations at Links of Noltland in Orkney are a rare example (Moore & Wilson 2011). In the end, the best examples, I believe, would be something like graves and I used the boat burial at Scar, in Orkney (see chapter 6). This did contain a set of Tafl gaming pieces (most likely the variant known as 'hnefetafl') but I widened my interpretation to include the entire site as a form of game, where the grave itself acted as a kind of board, lending meaning to the placement of people and objects within it. A game, of course, is active, and it is this sense of movement which animates it, gives it direction and a sense of narrative, yet the grave is also active while it is being created and there are many cases where the grave goods and bodies are manipulated and rearranged repeatedly, even after some time has passed (for example, Neolithic chambered tombs) and the grave has apparently been refilled and closed (Ucko 1969, Parker Pearson 1999. Mike Parker-Pearson's recent excavations at Cladh Hallan in South Uist have also demonstrated this aspect of burial); one of my arguments is that this is fundamentally playful or ludic.

David Kirsh (1995) has emphasised the importance of context and the relevance of the spatial distribution of things in space: space is not passive but part of cognition. This is also relevant to play, firstly, directly, in the sense that games like chess depend on a board to provide a quantifiable space against which the play unfolds and which helps to provide meaning, but also, indirectly, in the sense that all play takes place within a 'backdrop' whereby the activity as a whole is given meaning, even if it is transitory and self-referential. The school hall where we played euchre, for example, and the people taking part and helping with the tea and sandwiches, are all implicated here.

Extended Cognition

I find the relationship between players, gaming pieces and the board or playing surface very interesting. One implication of the way chess and euchre players use objects, whether cards or pieces, is that cognition is not contained, but distributed — my reason for stating this is that the players repeatedly used the gaming pieces to help them work out what to do; it was never the case that the disposition of pieces on the board simply reflected some internal model held in the players' minds but that the players worked with them in skilful ways, continually moving them, discovering new or unexpected connections as they did so. These discoveries then fed the next round of decision making. This is, I believe, 'active externalism' in practice (see Menary 2010). Clark and Chalmers' oft-quoted principle is relevant here:

'If, as we confront some task, a part of the world functions as a process which, were it done in the head, we would have no hesitation in recognizing as part of the cognitive process, then that part of the world *is* (so we claim) part of the cognitive process. Cognitive processes ain't (all) in the head!' (Clark and Chalmers 2010, 29)

Clark and Chalmers stated their case simply and convincingly; their theory can also be seen in the light of the movement away from the 'Cartesian' perspective, where cognition is understood to be locked inside the head, towards one where the environment is acknowledged as playing a significant role in mental operations including learning (Vygotsky 1978), navigation (Hutchins 1995) and the ascription of agency (Gell 1998), among others. For archaeologists like Colin Renfrew (2004) and Lambros Malafouris (2013), Merlin Donald's concept of 'external symbolic storage' (Donald 1991) has been particularly influential. For Renfrew, 'the symbol cannot exist without the substance' (2004, 25). Steven Mithen (1996) has also taken an interest, although the archaeologists' perspective is often an evolutionary one, more concerned with mental hard wiring than with ecological cognition as in the approach of Clark and Chalmers. If a criticism could be levelled at the more archaeological side of the debate, it is that it takes quite a static view of human– object interaction; it is more interested in objects as repositories for memory, and in that sense has simply shifted the field of operations out of the mind and onto the environment without accounting for the necessary interaction between the two. Malafouris is, I believe, a good recent exemplar of this kind of approach: his account invariably seems to draw on past instances of writing and counting with the material world (Malafouris 2013, see also Hutchins 1995, 369 for a similar view of earlier theorists). Hodder has taken a more nuanced approach, seeking to account for human/thing, thing/thing, thing/ human and human/human relations via a sense of 'entanglement' (Hodder 2012, 88).

Agency and Play

Much of the debate around cognition has focussed on person/object relations, particularly the vexed question of whether objects can be understood to possess agency in the same way that humans do. Gell (1998), for example, is happy to treat objects as possessors of agency, even if of a secondary kind. Latour (1999) prefers to attribute agency neither to persons nor to objects, but rather to the compounds or 'actor-networks' that are formed when persons and objects interact. Tim Ingold has taken issue with Latour's so-called Actor Network Theory, and indeed with the concept of agency in general, insofar as it treats actions as the effects of an agentive cause. For Ingold, persons and things are possessed by action, and their 'lines of life, growth and movement' are entangled to form what he calls a meshwork (Ingold 2011, 63). Ingold sidesteps the problem of agency by seeking to follow the flow of materials (Ingold 2011, 16-17) instead of becoming caught up in an obsession with the 'materiality of objects'. For Ingold, the question of agency is a red herring: the surfaces between things are the real sites of interest (Ingold 2011, 30-31). For my part I have avoided attributing agency to gaming pieces, seeking instead to talk of action by proxy (Chapters 2 and 6).

Awkward Objects

I encountered a confusion between materials and materiality (as described by Ingold) in my search for archaeological examples of play (chapter 7). Here, I describe the difficulty of recognising play in the archaeological record, and provide some examples of awkward objects, the things I could not say for certain were play– related, but which might have been. I divided these objects into groups. Some had no conceivable purpose and had not been modified but could be shown to have been brought into the realm of human activity — were they used in a game? Others had been altered in some way, but again had no known purpose. Miniature things — tiny battle axes, or quern stones — also seemed to be play-like, and some obviously utilitarian objects, a stone tool, for example, might have been recovered as part of a set (also known as a 'hoard', see Chapman 2000, 105-131, Bradley 1998), have been used together with other parts of an assemblage, have been involved with cognitive processes, and to have been deposited in a ritual manner, much as the kinds of material objects more usually associated with play, i.e. gaming pieces, can be.

A quality that many of these objects shared was *surface treatment*: quartzite pebbles had designs applied in lamp black, or a slab of stone was covered with small circles, and the effect is confusion: the surface treatment has obscured the relationship between material and materiality.

Play and the world

This study has led me to the conclusion that play is not as set apart as Huizinga claimed. In the case of euchre, I could see many ways in which this game has close links to the island community where it is played, in the sense that it is part of a Westray way of dealing with life; from this perspective it is difficult to draw a firm line dividing play from life. One of the striking elements, for me, of the archaeological evidence was the way in which everyday objects like stones or fragments of pottery were pressed into service as playthings before being abandoned and allowed to quickly become part of the background once more. I could also see how an interest in placement — an essential part of board games — could be broadened out to include, for example, an entire grave with all of its constituent parts. This has led me to see play and games not as set apart so much as simplified, or very clear, examples of the ways we get on with the world.

In moving around things, and in moving things around we constantly encounter the new. In particular, we are made aware of *space* in ways we can not predict (Sutton-Smith 1997, 87). We discover new relationships between things and between ourselves and the things, and we could not have made these discoveries if we did not engage with the objects. It is not enough to imagine the world or to hold objects such as gaming pieces in the mind: even the small number of pieces on a chess board encapsulate too much complexity. This is obvious when we look at play, and the way people play board games like chess encapsulate it perfectly.

Finally, if there is an overall theme here it concerns the relationship between play, objects and people. I no longer see play as set apart as some have theorised, and the ways in which people make use of objects for play now seem to me to be no more than particular examples of something more general. The ways that people use objects during play; the ways they are manipulated, used as proxies, thought with; the ways that people pay attention to the relationships between objects, and manipulate these relationships, can be found everywhere in daily life.

Chapter 2

Playing Chess

Introduction

This study has two very broad aims. The first of these is to arrive at a better understanding of how people play games, the other is to explore how this could be applied to archaeological examples and, given my background as a field archaeologist, I was already aware of some of the limitations and potentials of the archaeology. I knew for example, or thought I did (see chapter 7), that certain types of game are better represented than others.

Board games are a recurring element of many archaeological assemblages and so when it came to anthropological fieldwork, one of the first things I did was to start attending chess clubs. During 2008 and 2009 I carried out fieldwork among chess players in Edinburgh and Orkney. I had several reasons for choosing chess. To begin with, it is a very complex board game, one where players must implement tactics and strategy and which can demand a large amount of careful forethought from the players. I wished to avoid games of chance: I believed that a game of chance would be less revealing because the players would have less control over the game, however I now think I was wrong here — when I subsequently went on to look at a card game (chapter 3 below) I found it just as interesting. With chess, my reasoning was that if I could achieve a better understanding of how people play this game, I might be able to apply some of this to games of strategy in general. One further advantage of chess for me was the existence of clubs in both Edinburgh and Orkney. At the time my work involved a great deal of travel between these two locations throughout the year and it allowed for some continuity if I could take part in the same activity in both places, even if it was with different groups of people.

The clubs I spent most time in, the Orkney Chess Club and the Edinburgh Chess Club, were not the only ones I visited but they were the most convenient. The Edinburgh Chess club in particular has games taking place most nights of the week, although some sessions are devoted to children and learners. These clubs were open and welcoming to strangers, a reassuring feature when I was first introducing myself.

The clubs are very different. In Orkney, the club met once a week in the bar of the Stenness Hotel, whereas the Edinburgh Chess Club owns its own premises. In Orkney the venue could be noisy, raucous even, and once or twice a player had to ask for the music to be turned down. Players could order meals from the bar during play. Also, because games took place in public it was not unusual for non-players or people not associated with the club to take an interest (I had instructions shouted at me a few times). The Edinburgh club was usually quiet and orderly; the atmosphere was much more controlled and felt more focussed. Conversation was low and players circulated around the tables with the minimum of fuss. Of the two, I found the Edinburgh Club more productive, because there were more players to talk to and because I simply spent more of my time there. The Orkney club was also interesting but more so, I think, for the context of the play than for the mechanics of the play itself, which is what I was most concerned with at the time. During this fieldwork I focussed firstly on my own experience of the game and then sought to explore my thoughts though observation and direct discussions with others. As a result, my findings have, I think, tended towards the cognitive.

The rules of Chess

I do not describe the rules of chess here; they are widely known and in any case are not directly relevant to this discussion. It is enough to know the basics, I believe: a game of strategy played on a board containing a grid of 8 by 8 cells. Each player begins with sixteen pieces and aims to win by 'checkmate' — the unavoidable threat of one's king piece's capture. Games do not end in checkmate as often as is portrayed in popular media, however: draws are frequent, as are resignations. Each of the 6 different pieces (pawn, rook, knight, bishop, king and queen) possess different attributes so that, for example, the rook may travel any distance on the adjacent rows and columns while the bishop occupies the diagonals. Each piece thus has its own properties and potential for influence, which combine with the others to create a network on the board. This network is notional and based on what could be termed the 'affordance' (Gibson 1979) of each piece: its potential in the given situation plus its theoretical potential in the future as the pieces are moved. As one plays one takes account of all the pieces and tries to use or work around this continually shifting pattern.

I am not great at chess. There is a complex method of ranking chess players' abilities and my ELO rating (if I had one) would, I believe, be currently around the 12-1300 mark, if what I have been told by other players is correct. This means that I was usually (but not quite always) the worst player in any group, and I became inured to defeat by gimlet-eyed 12 year-olds whom I would not normally have spared a second glance. It is also fair to say that I can sometimes hold my own on the board, if only for a short period. My standard improved through practice however and I believe this also gave me a better insight than I would have had if I could not play the game as well. Participation has therefore, for me, led to greater insight.

Some Chess Background

Chess has been a part of western society since at least around 1000AD (Eales 2007). It was invented in India, probably around the 6 century AD or earlier, (Mark 2007, see also Murray 1913) and was brought to Europe via contact with the Arab/Muslim world

(Eales 2007). Along the way some of the rules have changed and new pieces have been introduced. There was, for example, an early version which used four players and dice may have played a part. Shatranj is an early variant which was adopted in Persia in the 7 century. The queen piece, one of the most powerful on the modern board, is a recent introduction, evolving from around the 12 century (the queen pieces seen in the Lewis chess set were, at the time, fairly new) (Yalom 2001). Several variations remain in use today around the world.

Chess has long since entered the English language and even those who do not know how to play use chess terminology and chess metaphors: it is common to hear the weak or manipulated characterised as 'pawns' in another's game, especially if they are deemed as worthless or disposable in some way. Those who play chess are stereotyped as intelligent, and introspective, sometimes as poorly socialised loners, who are overwhelmingly male; it can be used in literature or cinema, as a quick way to indicate qualities in a character. In Ingmar Bergman's classic film The Seventh Seal (1957) the hero plays chess with death for the souls of his companions. Here, each piece and its fate at the hand of death is directly compared to that of an individual. The noble character of the protagonist is also cleverly emphasised by his engagement in this struggle with death.

Chess has a somewhat equivocal standing in our own society: it is at once both obscure and ubiquitous; very many people have played the game, if only as a child - but it is played by a minority of adults and generally has a fairly low profile. The game and those who play it have seldom enjoyed a very high status, at least in the West. A famous exception is the world title contest played in Iceland in 1972 between the American Bobby Fisher and the Russian Boris Spassky, which took on a metaphorical role representing the cold war struggle between East and West (Alexander 1972); one other more recent instance where chess hit the headlines, though not to the same scale, was the contest between the reigning world champion Gary Kasparov and the computer known as Deep Blue in 1997, which the computer won.

Chess and Cognition

When I began this part of my study I already had an interest in cognition, and I hoped that I would be able to explore this side of play. I was pleased to discover, then, that board games, particularly chess, have had a history in studies of cognition since at least the 19 century (see Gobet et al 2004). These studies fall into two camps; those which aim to uncover how such games are played, and bearing in mind their complexity, it is clear that this is not a simple matter, and those that aim to use board games to answer questions concerning some other more general aspect of cognition such as the role of knowledge and the nature of its acquisition (Gobet et al 2004; 31). Simon and Chase's development of 'chunking' theory (1973), for example, which has been influential in studies of board game psychology, derived from research with chess and examined expertise. Their theory, that expertise was linked to the ability to rapidly identify the most important elements of a given situation or problem, has been applied beyond chess.

A board game like chess has many qualities which make it suitable for these kinds of study. Play is governed by a strict set of rules, there are usually only two players, every move can be recorded by notation, specific positions can be reconstructed quickly and easily. Many of the cognitive studies are interested in skill or expertise and in the case of chess there is a complex but very accurate method of determining any player's standard, the chess ratings system or ELO number, which places a player on a scale that starts at around 500 (beginner) and ends around 2800 (grandmaster). A chess player's ability can be found simply by asking what his rating is and very often, at club level, a match with a stranger will begin with this question.

Laboratory experiments have thus been devised to measure, for example, the times taken for various players to memorise a given text book opening or the rate at which elements are transferred between short term and long term memory. Positions are set up and exposed to subjects for set measured times. The accuracy with which the subjects reproduce these positions is assessed or their eye movements around the board are recorded and transcribed. The values obtained from these experiments are correlated with levels of expertise, age, sex and so on (see Gobet et al 2004).

This study has, however, taken a different tack. It is concerned more with players in their environment and has taken account of the context of play and the interaction between players. I have aimed for a more rounded appreciation of what takes place during and after a game of chess. In particular I was interested in the active nature of memory (Bartlett 1995 [1932], 200-2001, Ingold 2000, 148); here, it is revealed to be more of a process than a structure, skilled (Rubin 1988), but not necessarily reliable (Neisser 2009, Neisser & Fivush 1994, Hyman 1999, Hirst & Gluck 1999).

Chess and Memory

Play seems to be a very spontaneous activity, one which requires little forethought or planning and which can erupt from nearly any situation. Chess, however, seems to be the opposite of this. It is play, but is it spontaneous? Everything I knew, or thought I did, about chess before I began my study told me that chess is not spontaneous. It is supposed to entail slow careful thought, and I knew that the study of past games is important. One of my aims was to investigate the role of memory and to try and pin down how spontaneous or planned the game really is.

The Edinburgh Chess Club is nearly unique amongst chess clubs in Britain (there is I believe one other, in the south of England) in owning its premises, which are located at the west end of the New Town. The premises comprise a small flat, one largish room of which is devoted to chess while the rest of the flat is occupied by a live-in caretaker, who also plays chess and is an active member of the club. A visitor could not fail to notice the bookcases which occupy one end of the room. They hold a large number of books, each one concerned exclusively with chess. The books, for the most part, contain records of old games in the form of a simple notation accompanied by illustrations and some — usually sparse — commentary on who the players were, the circumstances of the particular game and on any interesting aspects of the moves.

For anyone with more than a passing interest in the game and who would wish to improve his or her standard of play past a certain level, books like these are essential. They are guides through the endless variations which are possible in a game; they provide the reader with the best response to a given situation and illustrate some of the consequences of a given move. The use of notation means that chess skills have progressed; it is not necessary to rely only on one's own experience of the game.

One aim during play, then, is to understand and learn from these old games so that they may be used again — as the saying has it, after all, those who do not learn from history are doomed to repeat it. In an ideal world a player would research his or her chosen line of attack, identify the major variations and the best responses and then utilise this information during play, thus leading to win after satisfying win on the board. Of course, one's opponent has exactly the same aim and may know the variation as well as, if not better than, you. For this reason a game can become, in effect, a contest of memory.

This is most relevant in the opening moves of a game. At this stage the number of moves which have been made is small and the number of possible moves is likewise limited. As the game progresses and pieces start to move around the board the possibilities increase so rapidly that it becomes impossible to rely purely on memory to decide where next to move and skill becomes more important.

My own experiences demonstrated the importance of memory, particularly in the early stages of play. Very often, where play was following a recognised pattern of movement on the board my opponent might identify it by its name, such as the 'Sicilian' opening, or would comment on a particular move, identifying the variation. This was always good natured and there was a tacit acceptance that one of us might gain the advantage through a better knowledge of one of these sequences.

It is even considered a good thing if a player makes use of established patterns of attack. Part of the challenge of the game is to research these openings and make use of them. A great player might go further and detect a variation which has never been used but the reality for every other player is that all of the openings have been known and mapped out for decades. The advent of notation means that each one can be found, together with commentary and put into practice on the board. A player who makes use of this body of information is not thought of as a cheat, someone who has taken a shortcut, but the opposite. It demonstrates that a player is serious about the game, has commitment and a certain level of competence. It is not in fact all that easy to make use of the information and may not help if one's opponent is much better.

In one case where I had researched an opening and then put it into practice this caused a small amount of interest both to my opponent and to an onlooker. As it happened, this opening (the 'Scotch' game), which is slightly obscure and currently out of fashion, was instantly recognised, partly because of historical associations with the club. It was clear that just as I struggled to remember the moves, so did my opponent and for a short time I was at a definite advantage. For a very short time it seemed as though I might win. Eventually, however, I could not sustain this pattern and my opponent, who was of a much higher standard, quickly capitalised on my mistakes.

It would seem that he who has the better memory should, if not win, at least be in the better position as the game moves beyond the opening phase and into the middle game where a player's competence becomes much more relevant.

There are many other ways in which memory plays a role in chess, of which the study of past games is a particular form. Here, a player can examine a past game in its entirety and run backwards and forwards through it at will, extracting useful, illuminating, elements. A player will also learn from his or her own games, of course. There are at least three ways of learning from one's own games:

- There is the experience of the game as one is immersed in it and involved with the flow of the pattern of pieces. This is very different from the distant kind of rote learning from books described above, yet no less important. It entails an engagement with the game since the moves can elicit both joy and despair and this emotional aspect undoubtedly affects one's perceptions.
- One can review one's own previous games. This is only possible to do in detail if the game has been recorded, which will only usually happen if it took place as part of a chess tournament. At these occasions competitors record their moves using a standard form of notation. Armed with one of these recordings, it is possible to reconstruct every move on the board.
- When a game is over the players will often discuss it between themselves, as well as with onlookers. There are usually only one or two stages in the game which are discussed but these are the interesting points, for example where something unexpected happened such as the balance of power shifting or where a player made a mistake. The players will reconstruct the position on the board and then run through the alternatives, moving the pieces around, perhaps to see how a player could have made a better choice or even just to relive the play if it was particularly good. If a player made some good moves the sequence will be examined closely, dissected so as to isolate when and why the moves were good.

Memory in Action

The role of memory in chess may appear to be quite static, a good example of the Cartesian model. The use of dusty old books, in particular, seems, on the surface at least, to exemplify a model for memory which is popular, mainstream even, in cognitive psychology This lends itself to controlled measurement and categorisation and explains the fascination which chess has held for that and related disciplines for such a long time. Chess is an activity which is ideally suited to more traditional styles of cognitive study. Every game can be broken down into its constituent moves. A game can be stopped at any point and analysed. A given position can be quickly set up. The game is also very visual — the pieces form patterns which can be quickly assessed and reproduced — and positions can be represented easily on paper. The board provides a small, well-defined, landscape or world and the game has a definite beginning and end. The rules are simple yet there are many levels and it can become extremely complex. The patterns on the board likewise appear simple at first glance yet they contain a great deal of information and thus also contain complexity. There is the pattern of pieces on the board and the pattern of moves each piece is capable of. There are future patterns — good ones, bad ones, and unexpected ones — which fade into the predictable distance. This is all set against a backdrop of time, or rather timing, and punctuation.

The memorisation and recall of chess openings is a case in point. This would seem to be a simple case where information is learned and, once learned, stored conveniently until needed. To begin with, however, a chess opening is not a simple sequence of moves but is more a framework around which a great many variations depend. A player will seldom have the opportunity to play out the entire sequence just as he or she might like because of the complicating factor of the presence of the opponent, who has their own ideas on where their pieces should move. It is more usual that the player will get in at most three or four moves in a row before the opponent recognises the variation and seeks to nullify it. The upshot of this is that the player feels his way through the moves, alert always for unexpected replies. Before too long, the game has developed or mutated into new territory and the opening is left behind. During this phase the player has had an overall strategic objective — the successful implementation of a given opening — but this objective has been broken down into constituent moves. At each stage, one or two or even half a dozen alternatives are presented and the player must reason, logically, which is the best. The players then must recognise and distinguish the overall strategic pattern from other similar patterns while at the same time remembering the variations within it. I would argue that it would be more useful here to talk of memory in terms of an 'unfolding', which would give the sense of something opening up and becoming more complex even as it is investigated. Rubin (1988) argued that memory is a skill; his analogy of a rat sorting through a waste paper basket could be applied here, where skill is necessary to sift and sort all the possible alternatives to find the best fit for the current situation. This is not the only aspect of memory which is revealed by chess.

When players wish to review any part of a game that has just finished they begin by physically reassembling the pieces as they were during the game. It is not always obvious which pieces were on which squares and the problem is solved at least partly through discussion, in order that a consensus is reached concerning the location of each piece. In my own case I quite often wanted to re-examine a critical phase — inevitably, where the tide had turned against me — in order to understand what had happened. I needed to review my decision making process but I could not do so without the pieces there in front of me. I needed to know why I made a certain move. Did I miss something vital? Could I have made a better move? Often, my need related to my opponent's actions. A move had been made, at some point, which had seemed innocuous to me but which had in fact proven decisive to my downfall. I needed to identify that move so that I could hopefully remember it for my own future games, or perhaps categorise it so that I could recognise its type again. My opponents were unfailingly generous and helpful with these exercises — they would help me to reconstruct the board as it was and then talk me through their own reasoning, pointing out as they did both mine and their own mistakes, showing where I should have moved and so on. What becomes clear through this is that the reconstruction of the game also involved a recollection and reconstruction of past thought processes. I never recovered a single move but a sequence, which had its own logic and sense of 'flow'.

We would begin by placing one or two key pieces back on the board in roughly the right location and then shift them slightly until they seemed right. Other pieces would follow until just enough were there and we could replay that section of the game; it was never necessary to reconstruct the position completely, using every piece which was on the board at the time, neither were irrelevant pieces removed from the board if they did not interfere. I found it quite difficult to reconstruct these 'vignettes' however my opponents seemed to find it easy and I believe they were always accurate. Once the first couple of pieces were in place it would usually be fairly simple to fill in the position around them because there was some logic as to where a piece should be to give it the correct relation to the key piece(s). The key pieces acted as markers, stimulating memory and helping to show where the next ones should go.

There are a few points I would like to draw from the above example:

- My first concerns memory as *reconstruction*. During an average game the pieces on the board will move around a great deal, creating many different positions all of which are temporary and which will thus last for a short time, even if they are studied intensely while they do exist. There is no reason why any one of these patterns or indeed a sequence of them should be remembered, unless the game is at a critical juncture, when more time will be taken to study the board or a move is made which is so unusual as to stand out. For most of the time, these patterns are forgotten; as Whitehouse has commented, after all, learning is a process of elimination (Whitehouse 1996; 106). In order to recover a past position the players are helped by knowing roughly where the pieces were and by a knowledge of what is possible and what fits or 'looks right'. In the case of the chessboard they are helped by the small scale and the exact rules by which the pieces interact. It is clear though that there is no guarantee that a position, or pattern, will be reconstructed exactly, and sometimes it is enough that a reconstruction, though inaccurate in its detail, demonstrates a principle.

- My second point concerns the cooperative or social side to memory. Where a position has been reconstructed and the flow of play examined from that point, it is unusual for one player to remember every one of both his and his opponents' moves. A player will most easily remember his own moves and help with his opponents' and together they will work out what happened. In this system, the necessary information is shared and it is uncertain or doubtful if the memory could be achieved by just one person acting alone. Hutchins (1995) described a similar system in his study of navigation at sea, one which he termed 'robust' on the basis that 'If one human component fails for lack of knowledge, the whole system does not ground to a halt' (Hutchins 1995, 223). The players prompt one another verbally and demonstrate their thoughts on the board by placing the pieces where they think they should go. This leads to my third point of interest here which is the physicality of memory and the way in which it is helped by having the board and pieces to hand. Holding the pieces and placing them on the board and moving them around to see how they look in relation to one another is important. There is something about having the pieces out there, in front of you, which helps. It is difficult if not impossible to do it all in one's head.

In one incident which struck me as revealing I was present where a player of moderate ability ('Dave') reviewed a game he had played and lost a few days previously at a championship, with the help of a superior player ('Colin'). The game had been played as part of a competition and so he had a full record of the moves played. Dave and Colin sat at the table and Dave used the record to run through the game from start to finish. Colin assessed each move and commented on how Dave – or his opponent – could have improved their play. What was really interesting to me though was how much of the discussion revolved around the emotional state of Dave and the presumed emotional state of the opponent. The bare record of the game could be unpacked to reveal whether Dave was feeling rushed, apprehensive or confident and so on. When Dave tried to remember why he had made a certain move this was linked to his feelings at the time; by remembering or re-enacting a move he also remembered those feelings and, conversely, when he tried to work out why he had made a certain move it helped when he could reconstruct his emotional state. Colin actively participated in this by directly asking Dave how he felt when he had made the moves. The discussion went further and encompassed the emotional state of the opponent. It was clear, for example that time was running out (all such matches are subject to strict time controls) for the opponent towards the end and he made some obvious errors due to being rushed and flustered.

Finally, if there is a thread which connects the above it is the concept of action or activity. Memory in and of itself often has passive connotations — this is memory as mere storage followed by simple retrieval — which do not fit well with the behaviour which I have witnessed and taken part in. I encountered memory as a cooperative, social, feat; something which unfolds or is unpacked as it is encountered and which is explorative and reconstructive and which is in any case difficult to pin down to just one of these 'modes'. It might be better to talk of remembering instead since this would give something of the flavour of a process — as opposed to structure — favoured by many commentators (e.g. Bartlett 1995 [1932], Rubin 1988, Neisser & Fivush 1994). This process is skilled and not easily contained in one individual's mind or even in one individual, but is linked or distributed (Hutchins 1995) with others and sometimes dependant on inanimate objects

I now want to explore the issue of memory further but from a different angle, one which was hinted at when I mentioned the physicality of memory, above. This leads me towards a consideration of the relationship between the players and their pieces.

Thinking with things

Chess is one of those games which seems to be purely cerebral. Every person I spoke to prized, revelled even, in this aspect of the game and I definitely detected a note of pride here. The game is complex and difficult and so it is fair to say that those who play it well either innately possess or have developed certain skills. There are tales of Grand Masters who can defeat many opponents simultaneously, without ever looking at a board. These stories, while true, refer to a tiny number of extraordinary individuals and I was concerned more with how the average person copes with the demands which playing this game places upon them. Is it really so cerebral? If it is, how necessary are the pieces and why are they there at all? The question, then, is: does the game take place in the mind or on the board? To put it another way, are the pieces on the board no more than an external representation of an internal model or is the relationship between mind and board more complex?

I never asked a player this question directly, partly because it seemed too obscure but also because players were happy to talk about the game in hand or chess in general but only in certain, quite concrete ways. However, I did ask players how they played the game and this led to an interesting insight which throws some light on the question. When asked, most players responded by saying that they tried to look two or three moves ahead at all times. In other words they envisage their best move followed by their opponent's likely replies, their own replies and so on. In this way they are able to look forwards and chart a course through the game by building a model of their own future actions as well as those of their opponent.

It would seem that the game must take place in the mind and the pieces and the board are used as a kind of notation by which a record of progress is kept. The state of the game on the board would then permanently lag behind the mental model held by a player by at least a couple of moves. This is however an idealised view, perhaps representing the state of mind of a player immediately before he moves a piece, when he has decided on his best move and thinks he can predict the reply. The reality is less clear-cut and there are factors which ensure that a player cannot get too far ahead of the board.

Accounting for the Opponent

To begin with, an opponent's actions can never be predicted with complete accuracy and so the game will not always follow the path it 'should'. Mistakes are also made — a player can, for example, very easily miss something vital and move a piece to a square where it is easily taken. The effect of this is that the player might think two or more moves ahead but he will be brought back to the board as it is now, constantly, as he is forced to assess and reassess the position. I found it striking, in fact, how much time is given to the board in solid concentration. Players scan it again and again, looking to see that nothing has been missed and to take account of the latest move and how that affects play. This was true even where very minor or obvious moves were called for. I was struck by the care which good players took over a move which to me seemed to be routine, the opening first couple of moves for example, which are made again and again and which, I assumed, would be made quickly without much thought. It became apparent that the aim was to avoid routine, to take each move as it came and not take the opponent's moves for granted. The way to do this is to use the board not as a static form of notation for what one already knows but as a continuous source for information about the game. The (good) player, then, learns about the game from the board and does not rely on an internal model.

For a player such as myself it is in any case impossible to remember the disposition of the pieces on the board. This is partly because the pattern keeps changing, sometimes quite quickly, and it is essential that the board is there between myself and my opponent so I can keep referring to it. In practice this means that I concentrate on the board and the pieces to the exclusion of just about everything else. I look constantly from piece to piece to piece, checking their positions, how they relate to one another and imagine the potential effect that a piece may have if it or others were moved. If I cannot keep the board in my mind I am forced to leave it out there in the world where it is not wholly under my control but subject to the will of others.

The relationship between player and board is therefore complex. The player must plan ahead and so formulate the tactics by which an overarching strategy may put into action, but the board constantly provides new information and so the tactics are constantly adjusted. The relationship is perhaps better visualised as a circular or cyclical one. There is a striking passage in Bruno Latour's study of science (Latour

1999; 59-60) where he describes the use of a Munsell soil book by a soil scientist. Here he remarks on how the seemingly simple task of assigning a colour reference from the book to a small sample of soil can only be achieved if the soil and the referent colour are immediately adjacent. It is very difficult to simply look at the soil, remember the colour and then look it up in the book. Latour makes the point that we distrust our brain; we do not have faith in it to remember a simple colour over more than a few millimetres. It may seem odd to compare this to chess yet it strikes me that the soil scientist and the chess player share something in the way that they distrust reality. If the soil scientist cannot remember a colour how can a chess player keep the game in his mind? The soil scientist tries to use his memory as little as possible to carry out this task and so he places the soil sample next to colour after colour until a match is found.

The chess player likewise does not rely on memory and so must search the board constantly — learning from it but essentially leaving it there, in the world. He tries always to think ahead of the board yet is drawn back continually and in effect his own thoughts advance in step with the movements of the pieces. The pieces are therefore not a mere external representation of an internal model; they are tools to think with and since this is the case it leads me to a consideration of the pieces themselves and the relationship between the pieces and the player.

I would also like to point out another way in which this process, where the chess player chooses which move to make, does not have to be so 'cerebral'. It is often idealised as a thoughtful game, one where the player runs through the options in his or her head before choosing the best move, yet there is room to take account of skill and of a more body-oriented approach. I believe that the difference between my own style of play, where I have to work out each of my options, may differ from better players in a much more fundamental way; these players are better because they play less with their mind and more with their body. Gobet et al (2004, 119-123) outline several laboratory experiments, involving chess players at various levels, which have demonstrated the 'instrumental' role of pattern recognition. As Gobet et al put it, 'pattern recognition underpins skill at chess' (page 122). This is also borne out by Kirsh and Maglio's analysis of Tetris players, which pointed towards the importance of pattern recognition as a speedy response to problem solving (reviewed in Clark 1998, 65-66). The good players navigate through the huge number of variations in the complex sections of a game in a more skilful fashion, making use of the patterns on the board in a way which is more physical or intuitive. Players at my level, by contrast, rely on brute force; like a computer, which has no skill, I must choose which moves are best by laboriously calculating the worth of each one. I believe I encountered this several times, at the Edinburgh Chess Club in particular, when I played opponents who were much better than I. They were skilful at detecting the worthwhile avenues amongst all the many dreadful ones, but to do this they had to either possess the ability to project the game forwards, in their minds, for a large number of moves into the future, or they had another system for coping with the choices. My opponents always denied that they looked more than two or three moves ahead, which is sometimes insufficient, but they did admit to a good grasp of the tactics; they knew what 'looked good' and got by on the kinds of incremental choices I could not detect. For example, a bishop might simply be moved one space to a position which was 'stronger', or the king tucked away behind some pawns. They could then capitalise on these good skilful choices as the game progressed, and I always seemed to find myself in a poorer position, where an innocuous move made several turns ago by my opponent now came into its own, and that bishop was now revealed as vital to my demise.

Materiality

In the Edinburgh chess club the room is occupied by 12 tables, each with a chess board set into its surface. These boards are permanently occupied by pieces; they are never put away but at the end of a game simple placed back on their squares ready for the next game. The pieces are large and quite heavy; they are made of plastic, or resin, and seem seldom if ever to have been washed. There is a thin coating of grime on them, missing only where fingers have kept areas polished through use but the actual condition or appearance of the pieces does not seem to matter. What is important is the game itself which is, as I have mentioned above, glorified as a cerebral pursuit, perhaps *the* cerebral pursuit above all others. It may seem strange therefore to consider the pieces as part of this study, yet the question here is, how do the pieces affect play?

Agency and Chess

Many recent discussions of materiality make use of the concept of agency (Giddens 1984, Barrett 2000) in a bid to understand how humans interact with things (e.g. Dobres & Robb 2000, Gell 1998, Miller 2005, Boivin 2008, Reed 2007, 35-39). Alfred Gell's 'Art and Agency: an Anthropological Theory' (1998) has been particularly influential. He posited that objects do in fact have agency, even if he assigned them a secondary level, but his use of agency is explicitly pragmatic — an object could be said to have agency as long as it was treated by those around it as though it did. This led to an interesting discussion of idols as well as to the claim that his car could be said to have agency because when it broke down he regarded it in terms of personality. Subsequent discussions have tended to focus on Gell's treatment of things as objects with agency without giving due consideration to the limitations which he himself placed on his theory, which was that it related specifically to *art objects* and that he wished to create an *anthropological* account for their treatment:

> 'The basic thesis...is that works of art, images, icons, and the like have to be treated, in the context of an *anthropological* theory, as person-like; that is, sources of, and targets for, social agency.' (1998; 96)

Given that the object of his discussion was to take a fresh look at *works of art* it becomes less clear whether Gell believed that things in general could be said to possess agency and it is interesting that he wished to restrict his interpretation to the realms of anthropological theory. John Robb (2004) has driven the discussion on by noting that agency entails both the effect of action and intention/volition/consciousness (2004; 131). As he puts it:

> '...if we want to understand how material culture acts upon humans, we should not look for it to have some quasi-human quasi-intentionality...material culture intervenes to structure human life through the genres, institutions, beliefs associated with them; because people cannot act in pure volition but necessarily experience and direct their volition through such fields of action, we necessarily structure our use of artefacts according to the field of action the artefacts are embedded in. In other words, humans attempt an agency of why; material things provide the agency of how' (2004; 133).

To bring this discussion back to chess, it is clear that chess players do not normally consider the pieces to have agency. I have never heard a player blame a poor move on the bad behaviour of one of the pieces. They regard the game as highly cerebral and suggesting otherwise runs the risk of creating offense. Robb's analysis is thus more relevant here since it is nuanced and takes account of the relationship between player and piece. If there is a pitfall it is with the way in which objects can here become reduced to tools; they become the means by which humans achieve their ends. In the case of chess it is by no means certain that this comparison is valid. It is debatable whether a chess piece achieves anything beyond its own being. It is used to occupy squares on the board, to apply pressure on other pieces; to take them; to act in concert with others in attack and defence and so on. In this sense it is a tool by which a game of chess is played, however that is all it does. It has no purpose outside of the game and gives rise to no product which survives the game, unless one counts the status of the player or perhaps the use of chess sets as status symbols. I have often seen chess sets displayed in the houses of people who will admit they cannot play but like them for their appearance, and perhaps for what they imply about their owner.

To enquire into the relationship between objects and agency presents me with a conundrum. On the one hand I have argued above that the game on the board is more than a representation of some internal model held in the mind of a player, and that the relationship between player and piece is more complex. If I follow Gell then the chess pieces possesses agency, even if only of a lesser order. If I follow Robb then I go to the other extreme and the agency is located entirely within the player and I must see the chess piece as akin to a tool: something functional, possibly abstract, by which a further aim is achieved. Both of these scenarios are unsatisfactory because they do not account for the behaviour which I have witnessed.

Arguments like Gell's or Robb's stem from the supposition that artefacts are embedded in human relations. This presupposes humans as 'material animals': creatures which exist and come into the world as part of that world and which are not artificially divided from it. Our relationship with the objects in our vicinity is dependent on our orientation or focus of attention. In the case of chess pieces, which happen to relate to the game of chess, our behaviour is changed when we take part in the game 'offered' by the presence of these objects. This point of view derives from a more 'ecological' approach (Gibson 1979) and is the product of viewing the individual as an organism which is engaged wholly with the environment and not as a mind which encounters it through the mediation of the body (Ingold 2000, 3). How might such an approach help us to understand the relationships between humans and things? Attributing agency to persons and/or objects seems more to cut them off from the world in which this agency is applied than to draw them into it, since the world itself is reduced to a field of agentive effects. How else, then, can we understand the relations between humans and objects, and the ways objects affect human behaviour? We need an alternative approach.

Action by Proxy

Bruno Latour (1999; 176-180) has noted how human behaviour is affected according to the nature of the objects around us and the possibilities offered by those objects. One of his examples was firearms; for Latour, human and gun combine to form a new composite agent; one which acts in unique ways according to the opportunities presented by the object. I could follow Latour and suggest that, at the chess board, there is a conjunction between player and piece. This could be best understood as something active and transitory; a process which is dependent on the presence of the player and affected by the possibilities offered by the piece.

This explanation would not be completely satisfactory, however. Latour's concept is easy to understand when the person is holding the gun, less so if one part of the composite is absent. In chess, for example, it was quite common for a player to rise from the table and go to the bar and order a drink or some food, or go to the toilet. When a player did this the game did not immediately crumble. The other player remained where he or she was and continued with the game, as if their opponent was still there in front of them, and yet no player ever spoke of the pieces as if they were independent or possessed agency. The key, I think, is that the players were engaged in a kind of action by proxy. Both had decided at the beginning of the game which were their pieces: at this point they had effectively agreed to treat the pieces as if they were the players, a necessary step if the game is to take place. Proxy action allows for these inanimate objects to be treated as if they represented others but without becoming mired in the question of whether they could be said to possess agency.

If the relationship between player and piece is understood in terms of proxy it helps to explain a few things about the Edinburgh Chess Club, and chess in general. For example, in one corner of the room was a glass case which contained several chess sets. These were not like those which were played with because they were figurative: the ones on the tables were all of the Staunton design which is mostly abstract (the knights are the only pieces which are less so). The chess sets in the glass case resembled people, gods, or fantastic creatures, such as Lord of the Rings characters. I never saw them used, but obviously there is a way in which chess pieces can be representational. The Lewis chess pieces famously represent real figures present in the 12 century, and they do so with a great deal of personality and humour. Modern players might wish to play down this aspect of the game, yet the pieces must represent them on the board and it is a short leap to see that they can also represent others.

Performing Chess

The game can also be understood in terms of 'performance'. Performance is a useful concept because it brings together several different strands, especially the ephemeral nature of play. However long a game of chess lasts, be it 20 minutes or an hour, once it is finished it is gone.

When the game has finished there is no product, no residue which can be easily identified unless one counts a slightly increased experience of the game or vaguely improved level of skill. Even where a game's moves have been noted down this is not the *game* but an imperfect record of what went on. It does not include many of the most important aspects: the thoughts and feelings of the players, their emotions, the setting and so on. My observation of and participation in attempts to reconstruct past games has emphasised for me how the movements of the pieces are tied up with these emotional aspects, which cannot be easily recorded but will re-surface as part of the process of remembering.

The pieces are not used as tools to create something else and they have no function outwith their participation in the game unless it is simply to *be* the chess pieces. As chess pieces they are available to take part in the game and it is during the game that their purpose is achieved. It is rather like a dance: a body movement which has its own internal logic, a beginning and an end, yet which only exists as long as it is being done. The game has the extra element of materiality (although a dancer may have a prop, and a predefined space to move in) which is provided by the pieces and this brings the game back to reality, in a way. It is a rather pure example of how we interact with the world, on a daily basis, and move on. The performance of the game is above all something which involves skill and practice and is an achievement which exists in the moment of its creation.

Chess, along with board games in general, offers a good model to think about how humans interact with the world around them. I believe that games like chess are particularly enlightening for studies of memory, as has long been recognised by cognitive psychologists, but also for studies of materiality and the relationships between humans and 'things'. A board and the pieces are 'pure' in a way that other objects are not because there is no product. The game is a performance which is dependent on things but when it finishes there is nothing left except memory. While it is in progress it throws the relationship between human and object into sharp relief.

Much is made of the complexity of a game like chess. It is a remarkable fact, given the simplicity of the rules and the small size of the board, that chess is one of the most complex games ever invented. It remains one of the few never to have been completely 'solved' by humans: for nearly every other game a strategy can be formulated at the beginning which will result in a known outcome (one other exception is the Chinese board game called 'Go'). For some games the solution is easy; a child soon learns how to play noughts and crosses so that a draw is always the outcome. For others, computers are needed to calculate the variations. In chess, where there are 'more pure strategies than the estimated number of electrons in the universe' (Binmore 2007; 37), a full solution has yet to be calculated. This complexity is, however, misleading if it distracts us from the fact that it is no more than one tiny part of the world we inhabit.

If there is one thing which I have taken to archaeology from this study of chess it is the idea that things are good to think with. This is especially important for archaeology because there is a tendency for archaeologists to see things – artefacts – as somewhat static or passive. Chess players use their pieces in many ways – as notation, as markers, as proxies, but always this is an active relationship and one that fails when movement ceases. My argument is that chess is simply a very good, very clear, example of how objects and humans interact.

It is this idea, where the movement and interaction with objects provides ways for humans to think and act that *could not otherwise be achieved* that I take to archaeology. The manipulation of the pieces on the board provides the players with information which can only be gained this way: not by thinking about it, or by reading about a past game in a book. I suggest that the movement of objects by people and the movement of people around objects is part of our cognitive engagement with the world and that this is fundamentally ludic or, at least, that games express and make use of a fundamental relationship between ourselves and the world.

Chapter 3

Playing Euchre

Introduction

In the previous chapter I discussed chess and my experience of the game as it is played in different clubs in Scotland. I found it difficult to engage with the players beyond the confines of the game and the walls of the club, however, and this had the result of throwing my study back on to my own perceptions of play. This chapter, by contrast, presents the results of fieldwork on a card game called euchre, as it is played by the people who live on the island of Westray in Orkney. Here, I have been able to study a game in context and have, over several years, come to know the various individuals who play the game as well as find out something about how people live their lives on Westray. Euchre also has the advantage of simply being very different from Chess and thus provides for different insights into play, to allow play to be seen from another angle. Given that my study is heuristic and explorative I view this as a distinct advantage.

In Westray up to thirty people come together to play an unusual, communal, version of the game, one where individual achievement is the aim yet at the same time this is set within a context of wider social good. It is a game which requires some skill to play well but which also incorporates chance, and the risk elements must be managed successfully if a player is to do well. I find the game is interesting in its own right as well as in terms of the light it sheds on wider aspects of Westray society, especially the manner in which risk is managed.

Euchre in its Context

The relationship between a game and the lives of the people who play it is always interesting. Play is ambiguous, resists definition and is susceptible to rapid change: key attributes which allow for its spread, in the form of various games and several authors have treated play as an activity which is both adaptive to and reflective of the 'host' society (Geertz 1993, Weiner 1988, Huizinga 1950, Sutton-Smith 1997, Guttman 1994). It is clear, after all, that games have a habit of being changed to better suit the place they are played. One well-known - perhaps the best known - ethnographic example of this is cricket and the Trobriand Islanders (see Weiner 1988, 114-115); here, missionaries introduced cricket in its standard form in the early 20 century with the aim of diverting the Trobrianders from the preoccupations of heightened sexuality and fighting, which dominate around harvest time. Within a short time, however, the islanders had altered and adapted the rules of the game in order to mediate these activities all the better. The missionaries' intentions had been subverted, and in the process the game had become something more approaching a ritual than a simple game of cricket.

There have been other studies which situate play within society: American Football and the United States (Guttman 1994); poker and the Inuit (Riches 1975); cock fighting in Bali (Geertz 1973). Huizinga, for his part, treated play as a fundamental building block of 'culture' (Huizinga 1950). There are some elements of euchre which have been adapted to local conditions, which will be described below. These are a further example of the way in which play can be used to suit particular agendas. Sutton-Smith (1999) has made the point that play is malleable, and adaptable and has shown how it is easily co-opted in various disciplines such as psychology, cognition, education and so on.

For my part, I have also sought to explore a game within the context of the lives of those who play it but I am wary of seeking any kind of causal relationship between the two. I do not, for example, believe that there are certain types of game such as games of chance or games of strategy which can only be played by people in agricultural societies, or by pastoralists, but view this as a kind of determinism which is very often linked to evolutionary notions according to which simple societies play simple games and as societies become more complex they adopt or invent more complex types of play (see Sutton-Smith 1997). Accordingly, I have avoided drawing these kinds of inferences between the ways that Westray folk live their lives and the ways that they play their euchre. I do not attempt to use euchre as a model for Westray society. There is a tendency with such studies to set play apart; it becomes the 'mirror', the marginal activity which somehow at the same time provides insights into 'proper' or mainstream society. This reflects, I believe, an inclination to regard some activities as more important, or more 'representative', than others. Play inevitably suffers in such schemes since it can never shake off its association with children and childhood.

At the same time I have been attracted by the ways that euchre *fits* Westray: I do not believe that the various types of play which are enjoyed by a society are played at random. There are innumerable games available at any one time, and a society plays those games which find a *niche* there, for whatever reason, and simply disregards others. Euchre, then, is simply a game which has found a home in Westray.

In this chapter I discuss euchre and the ways that people live on Westray. A characteristic of play is the presence of rules which control the flow of behaviour. It is the rules which serve to define the play and set it apart from other activities (Huizinga 1950). If one were to categorise play according to the level of control, a board game like chess would be at one end of the scale and play forms such as painting, or perhaps some types of children's play, might be at the other. Euchre would be placed closer to chess. Some activities on Westray are similar in that they are also quite rule-bound. Farming and fishing are two such: they are tightly controlled by outside agencies and the farmer or fisherman must take account of these rules as he (or she) makes a living.

Rules as Paths

My view of what to consider as rules has been quite straightforward: I have included such things as external, public, regulations without looking deeper for the hidden rules by which some private aspects of life are lived. My view of these rules is not so much that they form a structure so much as provide paths to be followed and that our engagement is an active one. The euchre player is enmeshed or woven into the rules and the play arises out of the movement of the game. Sheets-Johnstone states that '... creaturely movement is the very condition of all forms of creaturely perception; and creaturely movement, being itself a creature-perceived phenomenon, is in and of itself a source of knowledge' (Sheets-Johnstone 2011, 113). For Gibson, also, movement is implicated in our very interaction with the world (Gibson 1979). Movement provides the link between the rules and the game; it is this movement, this action, which generates the play and play is inseparable from movement. The players do not impose their idea of play on the world but follow its emergence through the game, as it is revealed by the cards.

The cards *are* rules; they provide directions and it is as if the players are following or being carried along a trail. Every so often they will hit a junction marked by a card. The card there will help the player decide which path to take. For euchre, a 'closed' game, the path opens or unfolds only as one progresses. The player cannot see too far ahead and cannot turn back, he is caught up within this process. The line or thread which can be traced through the movements is point to point, the play has been broken into a series of sections (Ingold 2007, 71-74)

I was interested to investigate the extent to which farming on Westray could be said to be rule-bound - much as games, like euchre, are rule-bound - and to see how people interacted with them, whether they were followed slavishly, and how farming coped. I was also interested in decision making and in how these decisions managed the risk element in farming, much as the decisions made in a game of euchre cope with the risk element there.

Risk

A number of authors have approached the subject of risk (Douglas 1985, 1986, 1992, Douglas and Wildavsky 1982, Beck 1992, Giddens 1999, see also introduction in Caplan 2000). A 'risk society', according to Giddens (1999, 3), is one which has become increasingly preoccupied with the future; this is the source of the risk, which must be planned for. Douglas and Wildavsky have developed Douglas' interest in risk and blame into a general theory whereby the perception of future risks, for example of environmental degradation, becomes a battle ground for individuals and groups with competing lifestyles or world views. More recently, Caplan's (2000) discussion has contrasted the sociological approaches of Giddens (1999) and Beck (1992) with that of

Douglas, and has noted the apparent lack of anthropological interest in the subject. At the time of Caplan's contribution, it seemed that risk was a subject which was about to come into its own in anthropology, according to Caplan, mostly as a result of the involvement of Giddens and the recent publication, in English, of Beck's magnum opus. The concept of a 'Risk Society', following Giddens (1999), seemed relevant and topical yet it seems to have faded a little since then and I have found it difficult to uncover more recent contributions to the subject.

In any case, Giddens, Douglas and Caplan understand risk as a forward-looking activity: behaviour is affected by perceptions of risk. The likelihood of a certain event taking place is appraised and people respond accordingly. My own understanding of risk is slightly different; from my own perspective I see risk activity less as forward-looking and more as a response, and in that sense it is also in fact backward-looking: people cope with the results of the decisions taken around risky situations and this is as true for the player at the card table as it is for the farmer. It is apparent that risk is *managed* on Westray and accordingly some people such as the farmers must take a long view. Managing the risk entails a kind of following, or fatalism – once a decision is made one allows the consequences to emerge and follows them to see what happens. Even so, Westray has a reputation in Orkney (I believe, generally a fairly conservative, risk averse place) for being a more 'go-getting' place. Westray farmers were some of the first in Orkney, during the 1970's, to adopt innovations such as slatted barns, which required large financial investments. One farm has recently installed a biodigester (Watts 2012); many others have invested rapidly in wind turbines, taking advantage of the higher Feed-In Tariffs available up to the end of 2012.

Playing Euchre

> 'No sedentary game is more popular, or so generally played for amusement in domestic circles, throughout the wide spread 'eminent demesne' of the United States, as Euchre – the Queen of all card-games...' (Meehan 1862, *preface*)

I enjoy card games and have played many but I had never heard of euchre before I travelled to Westray. The game does, however, appear to have a distinguished pedigree. It was played widely in the United States during the mid-19 century and is thought to have arrived in America with German or Dutch immigrants possibly via Cornwall, where it was popular. It is a descendant of a game played in Europe at the time, possibly Juckerspiel, an Alsatian game (Parlett 2004, Parlett 2013) or Ecarte, which was originally French. A relationship between euchre and Ecarte can be clearly seen, since both are trump games played by partners using only part of the deck. Ecarte itself is related to Whist, which is possibly the model upon which a large number of trump games are founded. Euchre is still played in America today, as well as in Canada, Britain, Australia and New Zealand (see Wikipedia entry on 'Euchre') and is currently enjoying a rise in popularity. My own experience suggests that it is not well known in Scotland outside Orkney, and even in Orkney it seems to be confined more or less to Westray. More recently, however, I have heard that euchre remains popular in the Royal Navy and is the card game of choice on board ship; I have also been told that euchre here can entail gambling and drinking, and fights have been known to break out during play.

The History and Rules of Euchre

The name 'euchre' has uncertain origins but Parlett has recently argued, convincingly I think, that it is a corruption of the 'Jucker' element of Juckerspiel rather than Ecarte, the more common explanation, and gives several early 19 century examples to justify this. He also suggests that the similarity of the spelling of 'Euchre' to 'Eucharist' may be a deliberate and later conflation (see Parlett 2013).

Some terms appear to be historical and relate to the game's origins in 19 century Europe. The Jacks are called 'bauers': German for Jack; the Jack of the trump suit is called the 'Best Bauer'.

Euchre is a card game for four players who are split into teams of two. Partners sit diametrically opposite each other and the composition of each team is traditionally decided by cutting the pack: the top two cuts form one team, the bottom two, the other. The lowest cut is the first to deal. The game is played for tricks and only part of a standard British/American deck of 52 cards is used: the 9 to Ace plus the joker (euchre is, incidentally, said to have been the game which first introduced the joker, as a kind of 'super trump'). The highest card during play is the joker, followed by the jack of trump suit. The jack of the other suit of the same colour is the next highest, then ace, king and so on. So, if hearts were trump the highest face card would be the jack of hearts, followed by jack of diamonds then ace of hearts, king of hearts and so on. The jack of diamonds has effectively changed suit and is for all purposes considered a heart.

The player to the right of the dealer cuts the cards and passes them to the dealer. Each player is then dealt five cards; the dealer moves around clockwise with each hand so that each player has a turn to deal. The cards are dealt in the order of first three then two cards, and the remaining cards are placed to one side with the top card turned face upwards so that everyone can see the card. The players now take turns to decide whether to 'make' or 'order up' that card as the trump suite for this round of play. This is a key point in the game and the decision rests on an assessment of one's hand. If a player has a good hand *and* is able to choose trump then he has a clear advantage (conversely, if a player has a strong hand in one suit but trump is chosen in another suit, which happens often, then one is at a definite disadvantage). This is also the point at which the player must decide whether, having chosen the trump, he will need the help of his partner or to 'go it alone' instead. If he thinks his hand is good enough to go it alone then he will gain more points, should he win.

Partners do not know the composition of each other's hands. The one time when a partner's hand is referred to is when a player chooses trump. At this point, the partner will look (sometimes slightly anxiously) at him, waiting to hear if the player will go it alone and hoping that the player chose the trump because his or her hand is exceptionally good. In Westray the player will often simply say that they will need a lot of help, in a self-deprecating way, as if they do not really have a good enough hand. The partner will then reply, usually with another self-deprecating remark about how poor their own hand is.

When a player decides to choose trump – by nominating the upturned card on the top of the pack - he or she will say 'I'll order that up'. The dealer must then take the face up card and exchange it for one of their own. By doing so, the player is asserting that he is confident that his side will win at least three tricks in the hand.

Scoring at Euchre

The scoring works as follows. If a team wins three or four hands then they score 1 point. If they win all five then they score 2 points. When a player goes it alone he can double his score, so 2 points for three or four hands and 4 points for all five, a 'clean sweep'. Four points is the maximum which can be gained in any hand. If the team which chose trumps does not win enough tricks they have been 'euchred'. It is definitely a badge of shame to be euchred; it implies poor judgement on the part of a player, or poor choice of cards during play. In any case, fate has delivered a cruel blow and fortunes have been reversed. In the standard rules for euchre the game continues until eleven points have been gained by one side. Then the players can start again or perhaps move around so that everyone has new partners.

Playing Euchre on Westray

There are aspects of the game as it is played on Westray that are unusual. Firstly, it is no longer played in peoples' homes but in the community hall where up to thirty play together in organised sessions. It seems that it was once played in peoples' homes but this more or less died out at least twenty or thirty years ago and this more communal version is now the main way to play. I have not been able to trace the reason for this shift; certainly, it coincides with major building work to the school, which gave rise to the present location of the community hall as part of the school. The game has been played on Westray for many years, and many people who attended the games in the community hall told me how when they were young it was common for people to play at each other's houses in the evenings (this would be before mains electricity reached Westray in the late 1960's); however there no longer seems to be the same tradition of playing at home except on the very odd occasion. My impression is that euchre had faded somewhat before it was consciously brought back, as an event which could both make use of new community facilities and serve as an excuse to bring together members of the community who did not see each other as much as they would like, even on a small island. It might be more accurate to say, however, that people do not always meet each other on the island under the circumstances they would prefer. It may be difficult to avoid people yet it is also difficult to meet friends in the type of relaxed, communal setting which euchre provides. It is also true that a certain degree of nostalgia is fashionable among the older residents of Westray, for the days before mains electricity and before the regular short ferry services which now make life on the island so much easier but which have also changed it so much. In those days, the ferry to Kirkwall took some six hours and visited several other islands on its way. It called into Gill pier in Pierowall, where cargo was lifted off with a crane. Ferry visits were special, anticipated, occasions and many would gather at the pier to see it arrive. The ferry is now daily, direct, and takes one and a half hours; it leaves from a purpose built ro-ro terminal at Rapness, several kilometres to the south, and it is possible to spend a day in Kirkwall and be back on the island in time for tea. I believe that for the older Westray folk euchre comes from these older times; it is a kind of hangover from more sociable days.

The game is now played on the first Friday of each month, during the winter. I could see that euchre had been situated within the community in such a way that it fitted in to the farming year, a clear indication of euchre's assimilation and also that it might have other points of contact with life in the community beyond the game, particularly farming. The timing element was thrown into sharp relief one evening during late 2012 when for some reason we were forced to play on a Saturday night rather than a Friday night. Suddenly there was a group of six or eight individuals there whom I had only rarely or never seen at a euchre night before. These were mostly teenagers who had spent the week a ferry ride away at the school in Kirkwall. One or two were regulars who had been unable to attend the euchre when they reached the age when their studies took them off island (Pierowall Junior High school teaches pupils up to the age of 14. If they wish to progress then a pupil must attend Kirkwall Grammar School, which is residential from Monday to Friday. A feature of life on the island is the return of the children on the Friday night boat and their leaving on the Sunday night). Their presence changed the dynamic markedly: the average age dropped suddenly and it definitely became more talkative. During that session there were many comments on how good it was to see all the new faces, and the new faces remarked how much they missed not being able to come to euchre on a Friday night. There was a vote then to see how many wished to change to a Saturday, however the motion was defeated because there were too many other activities which would clash with a change. The euchre seems to slot quite neatly into life on the island and it is difficult to move it from its current location.

When I first attended a euchre evening I had done my research and expected to take part in many separate games. I knew that it was a game for four players and that a normal game does not last very long, only until 11 points have been gained by one side. I expected to finish one game and then perhaps move to another table and meet new players and so on. Instead, I found that a few key rules had been changed and that play had been broadened out to include everyone in the room in one massive, prolonged, game which started, typically, at 7.30pm and continued until a set number of rounds of hands had been dealt, usually by around 11pm (by which point I was very tired and my head was reeling). The usual way of playing, between four players, has been broken down and reformed so as to accommodate as many as will turn up on a night.

Two long rows of tables are set out in the community hall. As people enter the room they generally take the nearest available seat; men sit on one side while women sit on the other. Play still takes place within groups of four, at a table, as in the standard rules for euchre, but now play within each group is restricted to four hands: one for each person as dealer. Points are then totaled and winners and losers determined. The players remain seated until everyone has finished their game, when there is a shout of 'shift!' Winning men then move clockwise two seats and the winning women move anti-clockwise two seats. The losers stay at that table but move to the seat on the left (men) or right (women). It is possible, if one is a very poor player, to remain in one seat for pretty much the entire evening but most people circulate around the room, completing at least one circuit.

This continues until twenty four games have been played. There is a break for tea and sandwiches at half time, when twelve games have been reached. The tea and sandwiches are served by a group of three or four women, who have been preparing the refreshments while everyone else plays the game. The same women do this each session; they never actually take part in the euchre and not all of them even know how to play the game. They help, I think, partly because the game is played ostensibly for charity - a small fee is paid by everyone to the RNLI, a popular island charity but also, I think, because the euchre is seen as a good thing and it is as sociable for them, in their way, as it is for the players, in our way. In play terms they are an interesting oddity since they do much of the organisation and make the game possible. Thus they are more than mere spectators (not that they actually observe the game) for they also share in some of the benefits of the game.

At the end of twenty four games everyone's cards are collected and the winners declared. The man and woman with the highest scores will then each win a prize, which is always gift wrapped, to preserve the surprise; this is usually a pack of coloured pencils or a bag of sweets.

There is something collective about euchre on Westray Euchre. Individual games have become subsumed into one giant euchre session, which lasts until a certain number of games have been played, irrespective of the time (I have often stumbled, exhausted, out of a Euchre session long past 11:00pm, the last few games a complete blur). The game has also been moved from peoples' homes into the community hall, where everyone can claim equal access.

The place of Euchre in Westray

The similarity between the name for this card game — Euchre — and 'Eucharist' may not be accidental, as Parlett (2013) has noted. In the context of Westray, it brings to mind other interesting parallels.

To begin with, Westray's communal version fits very well in a place which values the church, and church attendance, very highly. Euchre, which is at heart a game of risk, has been moved out of people's homes into a public environment, where the goings on are subject to communal approval. No alcoholic drink is taken during euchre; the refreshments are reassuringly acceptable to all ages and would not be out of place at events held in the church. The presence of the ladies who prepare the tea and coffee and sandwiches is also reminiscent of the church hall. The game is communal and inclusive and the participants donate money to charity at the beginning of the evening. The way in which men and women are deliberately separated during play, by being placed on opposing sides of the tables reminds me of the way men and women would at one time have been placed on different sides of the church. There is gambling — it is a game of risk and we all play for prizes — yet the prizes are deliberately slight and token. It is as if this game, which can entail gambling, drinking and fighting (as with the Royal Navy) has been taken into the Westray community but tamed. It has been deliberately altered to appear respectable, perhaps to counteract any lingering doubt there might be over cards and gambling.

There is also another parallel with the church on Westray in that it was once fractured and divided into many small congregations (when on Sanday, a neighbouring island, I was told that each island's problems could be summed as: 'Westray had poverty and the Kirk while Sanday had poverty and drink'). The church on Westray is now much more unified and inclusive, with a smaller number of congregations who will take part in communal services.

The Players

A range of people take part in euchre, including 'incomers' (those not born on the island but now living there more or less permanently). One thing that struck me repeatedly was how well people know each other. The islanders grew up together, went to the same schools together and many are related in one more or less distant way or another. As a result, they know each other's strengths and weaknesses extremely well. Many of the euchre players have known each other for sixty or more years. Their familiarity is visible not so much in any extrovert way but more in a certain kind of manner. In the case of the card game I do not think that it is like poker, say, where players are reputed to read their opponents as much as the odds of the cards. It is more that they can account for each other's behaviour.

They know how to get on with one another, which is especially important on a small island, where it is difficult to avoid people. I often suspected that one person might not (or should not) be all that keen on another yet usually found it difficult to say this with certainty. There are very few individuals on the island who will say outright what they think of another — to an incomer like me, at any rate. This is even true where an islander has been the victim of another's 'meddling'. This diplomacy is occasionally frustrating and the two or three individuals who do say exactly what they think have been very useful to me in my studies, yet they are in some ways outsiders themselves, due to their candid speech. The difference is probably to do with where they speak. There is one man who will give you his opinion there in front of others and not care who hears, and is consequently thought of, I think, as something of a 'wild card', unpredictable. A couple of others will also let you know, indirectly, when no one else is near. Also one must not forget that there are odd blind spots in this picture of an island population where everyone knows everyone else extremely well. There is one individual, at least, who was born there and has lived on the island for 65 years but is considered a bit of an unknown quantity — due to his behaviour as a schoolboy 50 years previously. During one crisis where police were involved, I was asked, as an incomer, for my opinion of this man's character by other locals, who had known him at school, which I found odd.

In any case, when people play euchre they are relaxed and good natured but also alert, focussed and attentive to the game. It is expected that you will give your attention to the game, at the risk of drawing (mild) comments. One or two will direct quizzical looks, or worse, a kind of flat eyed stare designed, I think, to encourage the transgressor to do better. Beginners, however, are always treated with extreme kindness, generosity and forbearance. Beginners are apt to find everyone around them taking looks at their hand and advising on the best card to play. The other players will happily advise a beginner on how best to beat themselves.

A small number of incomers play euchre on Westray. The attraction of the game for an outsider is fairly obvious and openly admitted by most participants. It is an enjoyable way to spend an evening and it is also a way to meet people, which is important if one is an incomer to a place like Westray where it can seem as though everyone, though friendly, is caught up with their own lives. It provides a way in, an entry to a more social side of life on the island. Meehan (1862) commented on how social a game this is. According to him, if invited, one should make every effort to attend a game since not to do so 'risks ruining 3 other peoples' evening'.

How to win at Euchre

What are the *attributes* of euchre? I have described the rules, but *attributes* are different. If the rules provide a framework or a series of pointers for action, this is more to do with the shape created by the rules. Also, the attributes are more to do with the way the game is experienced by those who play it. The attributes are generated by the active engagement of the players with the game. Or, to put it another way, attributes are to rules as properties are to materials (Ingold 2011, 19-32).

Euchre is not exactly what might be called a 'wild' card game; at least, not as it is played in Westray. Poker is. Poker players risk all on the contents of another's hand. A poker player might lose hundreds, even thousands of pounds on one hand, or their house or car. A euchre player looks forward to a packet of coloured pencils, if favoured by lady luck. The difference is that poker is well suited to gambling, and euchre is not, even if both are games of chance.

The element of chance is one obvious important attribute, which comes to the fore in many card games. It stems from the original shuffle and deal of the cards at the beginning of play. Players can never know what cards their hand will hold before play begins and will only discover the contents of their partner's and opponents' hands as play progresses. In this sense, euchre can be characterised as a 'closed' type of game: important information is concealed from the very start but will eventually be revealed. Chess, by contrast, might be characterised as 'open': all information is always available.

In effect, the closed nature of a game like euchre provides an aspect which a game like chess is missing. A euchre player plays with the probabilities of what may or may not be present in his opponents' and in his partner's hands. As the game continues one gradually discovers — or perhaps has confirmed, if one has the statistical know how — where each of the cards is lurking. This element of uncertainty is really all about risk and the management of that risk: how does one play in a situation where one cannot possess the information needed to make good choices with certainty?

Following the Cards

When I asked euchre players how they coped with not knowing where all the cards were I was most often met with the reply that they simply 'followed the cards'. One or two try to work on their knowledge of the pack and where cards should be: for these players it is possible to make educated guesses as information accumulates during a hand. The problem, though, is that a player must be able to calculate the odds extremely quickly because the hands are played as fast as possible. Hanging around, or hesitating in order to calculate, is frowned upon because it disrupts the flow of play. There are other ways in which the tempo is kept up — there is the pressure of surrounding players waiting for tables to finish so everyone can move on to the next game and there is the presence of one's opponents and partner: they also all want to just get on with it.

Ultimately, I believe that 'following the cards' is a key to euchre and to much else about Westray life. Once a hand has been dealt there is only a limited range of options for a player, at least in most situations. As long as one 'follows the cards' (which I was advised to do many times) then the choice of card to play is usually straightforward.

There are certain people who are recurrently at the top of the league, who score better and who win the prizes time after time. These players do this partly by adhering to simple strategies, for example only 'ordering up' the dealer when they have certain card combinations in their hand. The thing is, there are a few situations which crop up repeatedly where it pays to have ones strategy in place, thought out, and ready, because when these situations arise there is not much time for action. A case in point is at the start of a hand, when the dealer leaves the card on top of the pack facing up and each person has the opportunity in turn to nominate that suit as trump. One strategy is to be bold and choose the trump when one gets the chance: know the odds and stick to them.

Once play begins one simply uses the cards available. As long as one follows the rules then the choice of cards is usually fairly clear; in fact in any given hand there are few meaningful decisions to make, it is a question of just playing out the variation and seeing who has won and who has lost.

Westray: A brief Introduction

The aim of this section is to introduce Westray and its people and to say something about how people live their lives there.

Location

Westray is one of Orkney's outer northern isles. It is situated to the north west of the Orkney archipelago and though small in absolute terms — it measures only some 7 miles East West by about 3 miles North South — it forms one of the largest in the group.

The island is remote and awkward to travel to, involving more than one ferry or flight from the Scottish mainland, but Westray maintains good contacts with the outer world. Around six hundred and fifty people live there; the population currently seems to be stable and even to have risen slightly in recent years, although levels are low compared to the middle of the 20 century when some two thousand people lived on the island. There is one village, called Pierowall, three shops, and one hotel. Westray is unusual in being able to support its own bakery, other islands in Orkney having lost theirs many years ago. Sanday, a nearby island of comparable size, lost its bakery during the mid-1980's as the population there fell below the level where it was economic. Contact with the outside world is achieved via a 'roll on roll off' ferry terminal at the south end of the island and by an airfield at the north end. Ferries are regular and take 1hr 25mins to reach Kirkwall, the capital of Orkney. It is possible, just, to live on Westray and work on Mainland Orkney.

Economy

The mainstay of the economy is farming, even if fewer are employed here than used to be. Prior to the advent of mechanisation following the end of the Second World War a great many people were needed on a farm because the work was highly labour intensive. The use of horses, in particular, required a great deal of labour (Fenton 1978). Farming also, of course, influences the appearance of Westray. At present, most of the island is down to grass and there is no apparent difference between one field, or plot of land, and any other, though there is a large area of hilly rough grazing at the western end of the island. Westray can be regarded as one giant farm, one enormous grassy field subdivided by six-strand fences, and many people have commented as such to me.

Until very recently fishing was a major activity on Westray with up to seven boats landing their catches at Gill Pier during the eighties and nineties. Westray is also said to have been a significant landing place for the 'black fish' at that time. Each boat would employ several crews – boats can be kept at sea constantly, swapping crews over every couple of weeks or so. Fishing is still a significant source of income, even though only one white fish trawler currently calls at Gill pier. The drop in the number of boats over the last ten years is said to be due mostly to outside factors, principally the enforcement of fishing quotas and the introduction of a licensing system for trawlers. Economic and social connections to other boats, based elsewhere, remain however, and there are other fishing activities, other than trawling for the white fish. There is a fish processing factory which employs some twenty people and deals mostly in crabs and shellfish for export to Spain and the Far East. This is the largest employer on the island. There is also a separate fish business which takes the fish that are landed and distributes them onwards to clients in Mainland Orkney. Several creel boats fish for lobster around the shore of Westray; the lobster from the various boats is handled by one company, which collects the creatures and keeps them in tanks before onward shipment as far as the London market. There is also a salmon farm in Westray waters; this was recently sold by local owners to a multinational (Norwegian-based) company.

Farming and fishing are the main sources of outside income but there are also a number of small businesses, some of which function mostly within the local economy, such as a builder who employs around half a dozen. There are also several jobs associated with the island infrastructure: a doctor's surgery, a school, two post offices, roads maintenance, a water treatment plant and so on.

Tourism is an expanding part of the local economy. Many people are affected directly by tourism or make a living from it. There is a local tour company and a heritage centre. There is one hotel and a number of holiday cottages as well as more basic hostel- type accommodation. The shops also benefit and there are two galleries selling a range of art work and gifts. Tourism provides a fairly dependable income for those involved but it is only viable during the few summer months. It is however a significant and growing element of the local economy (REC Consultants 2016) and is widely recognised as important for Westray's future economy. In this sphere of activities the islanders are able to project their own version of their lives and of the place they live in to others. Tourism to Westray is based on a perception of the island as friendly, unspoiled, remote and heritage rich. It can be said that they promote those aspects which they think will attract custom but it is also true that there is a sense of pride in Westray. People are conscious of their place on a small remote island; they are also well aware that parts of it are beautiful and they value their community extremely highly.

The Church

Finally, a large proportion of the population attend church regularly. There are at least four separate denominations which maintain churches on the island: Gospel Hall, Church of Scotland, Baptist and United Free Church. The Church of Scotland has the largest congregation and is undoubtedly one of the most important institutions on the island.

Risk Management

Westray is widely considered to be a confident, forward-looking place, both on the island and elsewhere in Orkney. Sometimes this is visible in small ways such as pushing for the funds for a swimming pool. Other innovations have been more expensive and have created a bigger impact. The Westray Development Trust, for example, has recently developed a community owned wind turbine, the first such in Scotland. The money which this earns will undoubtedly bring more changes to the island as it is used to fund various projects for the community. Westray was also a leading contributor to the Islands on the Edge initiative, which drew attention to the fragile state of these small communities all over Scotland.

Up until fairly recently (1990's) it was unusual for outsiders to move to the island, unless through marriage. Houses were not generally put on the open market but were sold to other islanders. In the last 20 years or so this has all changed and there are a lot of incomers now. The island is becoming increasingly diverse in terms of both the background of the inhabitants and the sources of their income.

The relationship between the islanders and the outside world is not always straightforward, and I encountered many cases where fledgling businesses were hampered by outside influences. These examples were not directly related to farming but they illustrate the outcome of a conflict between rules and the behaviour of the individuals concerned. In each case the individuals could not follow the rules and in effect their activity was forced to cease, much as those who play a game must stop when there is disagreement over the rules.

There are many individuals on Westray who are well able to initiate surprising and unexpected projects and there is a level of confidence on the island which encourages this kind of thinking, even if not all the schemes which are started eventually succeed. Sometimes a plan can be brought down by others' jealousy or when others feel that their own rights are being infringed. Sometimes there is a conflict between the islanders' own view of their environment as unspoiled and containing abundant resources and the view of others that these resources must be preserved. One way to characterise this might be as a system where individuals constantly innovate but within a system which has many checks and balances.

People on Westray generally get on with one another, however there is also (perhaps unsurprisingly) a certain amount of gossip. I have often discovered how one farmer is doing by speaking to another at the opposite end of the island. There is no police presence, and a lack of any need for one. Conflict resolution is mostly kept small scale and local.

Farming on Westray

Farming is the mainstay of life on Westray and it is to farming that I now turn in order to understand how euchre fits in with living on the island. My intention is simply to discuss those areas which have resonated with my study of euchre. This discussion rests on interviews with several Westray inhabitants, not all of whom are farmers, as well as two who have recently sold their farm and left the island for good. The interviews were based around a desire to understand how farming works, both generally and more specifically on Westray itself. Then, having identified interesting areas which seemed relevant to euchre, I followed these up with individual questions targeted at specific answers. This was not an exact process and I often found myself lobbing odd sounding questions at someone wherever I happened to encounter them, for example at the shop or in the middle of the road (for instance asking an old fisherman for details of the games he played while at sea). One consequence of this process is that this ethnography is somewhat abbreviated: I did not wish to understand everything but only to gather information on that which I thought relevant.

As part of this exercise I have tried to quantify how many 'farms' or farmers there are on Westray but found it not so easy. I have counted to around thirty but I cannot be more precise with this number because I have found that who owns land and who uses it are tricky questions. In one case, I have found that the man I thought owned and farmed one farm in fact rented all of his land to another. The owner, however, retained his 'quota' (calculated on a combination of area of land and average yield between 2001 and 2003) and continued to claim his subsidy, but on land now rented in mainland Scotland. This farmer has become a 'slipper' farmer, one who claims his subsidy from the EU (Common Agricultural Policy) but does not actively farm his land. He has never seen the land he rents in Scotland. There are other farmers on the island who own and farm their land in the traditional sense but who still rent small plots of land in faraway places, in order to boost their quota to a minimum level. This is considered good, normal, farming practice and has come about as farmers have adapted to the imposition of new regulations put in place a decade ago, which is not to say that the farmers actually like them. They find them bizarre, difficult and confusing, if ultimately rewarding. These regulations, known as the 'Single Farm Payment' (SFP), changed in April 2015 and farming is thus presently in a period of uncertainty.

Rules for Farming

The CAP sets limits on farmers' actions: payments are not dependent on the animals but on land and a farmer must maintain his land in good agricultural order if he is to receive his subsidy. There are many other regulations which control farming. All cattle, for example, have a 'passport', which is issued by the BCMS (British Cattle Movement Service) and which remains with the cow for life. The passport allows for the movements of animals to be traced, and no animal may enter the food chain without it. The death of an animal on the farm must be notified to the BCMS within 7 days. Every cow must be tagged and these tags change colour throughout its life. It is possible to judge the age of a cow simply by noting the colour of its tag. None of the farmers I spoke to were particularly happy with the level of regulations they were forced to comply with, seeing them only as hurdles to be crossed if they were to maintain their livelihood and much of our conversations revolved around the expression of a range of emotions, from mild bafflement or astonishment to outright anger concerning these regulations. The farmers present themselves as somewhat set apart from Mainland Scotland, or even Mainland Orkney. Some of the regulations, such as those intended to control the transmission of diseases such as BSE, Foot and Mouth or Bluetongue, are seen as really being there for others, with the implication that Westray and Orkney is a clean unspoilt environment, free from the types of disease more commonly found elsewhere in Britain. Given that these diseases have not been found here, it is arguable that the farmers are correct, but these regulations protect Orkney from the outside world. Others, such as the CAP, are seen as absolutely essential if farming is to continue at all on Westray. There are many on the island who look to the forthcoming changes to the SFP with trepidation. I know of one farm which has been sold in the recent past (sold during 2012) because the farmer and his wife felt very strongly that there was no future in farming. They have now left the island and are no longer involved with farming.

Selling Animals

The main source of income for a beef farmer, aside from the SFP received from Europe, is derived from the sale of his 'kye'. I had assumed that the farmers simply sold off those animals they did not want each year, keeping the remainder to breed more. I have found that the process, as it has been explained to me, is slightly more complex.

To begin with, when I asked a farmer how many cattle he owned (something I rarely did directly, since it is a slightly sensitive subject, and considered intrusive or vulgar, a little like asking someone what salary they earn) I would get a different answer to when I asked how many he kept. This is because a farm will keep a core herd of say 85 cows from each of which he will aim to breed one calf every year, although a certain number will be infertile at any one time (a farmer who can keep the infertile percentage below 10% is considered to be a good stock keeper). Many farmers have more than one bull, each of a certain breed, for example Charolaise or Simmental, and will aim for so many offspring from off each type. The various offspring are intended for different purposes. Some will be kept to replace cows lost from the core herd; others will be sold on at 6 months to other farmers who will invest the time and money in raising them to 12-18months, when they are sold for meat. Finally, a Westray farmer will also keep some of his animals until he can sell them for meat. There are no farmers on Westray who specialise in any one of these aspects of this type of farming, as is common elsewhere, for example on mainland Scotland where some farms specialise in buying in calves from other farms, to fatten for meat production. The risks, which would be greater for a farmer on Westray if he specialised, are dealt with by a form of diversification. In addition, all the farmers I have interviewed put their animals to market gradually in small groups. The aim here is specifically to spread the risk. It is not that a farmer sets out to achieve a great price for his beasts, welcome though that would be, so much as that he aims to avoid any great swings in price. If he put them all to market on the same day and the price was low then he would lose out. This strategy appears to rest on a desire for stability. A farmer could be lucky and put all his animals to market when the price is unusually good but he would rather not gamble. By putting them to market gradually he gains a more average price and the process is less risky. In addition, the cattle are spread further according to whether they are sold as meat, which would take place towards the beginning of the year, or to another farmer as stock, which would take place towards the end. The comparison with cards is obvious: if the cows were cards, some are being played as soon as possible, others are being held back for a greater income at a later date. If each animal were a bet, the bets are spread to achieve a better average.

Farming regulations

If Westray is often seen as a go-getting place, how is this possible if life is controlled by the CAP regulations, and animals are sold in such a way as to avoid the wild fluctuations which could be disastrous but could equally be beneficial? The answer is that Westray farmers adopt other strategies. Change might seem slow but it happens; there is a slow shuffling of land between farms. Some grow to near legendary proportions (for example the Brough Estate post war); others dwindle and are snapped up by other landowners. The aim of the game is to maximise yield through the acquisition of land and thereby to increase numbers of animals.

Regulations such as the CAP seem to be so powerful and all-encompassing that they should control farming completely, however the farmers do not see themselves as without options. The regulations are exact and must be adhered to but I argue that they form a framework, a system around which the farmers order their lives. The framework seems to be a straightjacket but if one factors in a timescale, one can see that the mass of regulations can be teased apart to be revealed as more of a set of rules, as in a game, which are used as pointers. The farmers live their lives in the time between the rules; the rhythm of their lives is dictated by the tempo of the rules-in-application.

Decision making for Westray farmers is undoubtedly based on perceptions of future risk, and in that sense theirs may be termed a 'risk society' (Giddens 1999). The conflicts, in Douglas's sense, are more between the farmers and their way of life on the island and the politicians and 'Eurocrats' who seek to control their livelihood from afar. The farmer's perceptions of risks are I think dependent on several factors: the quality of his land for example, or the availability of sons or daughters to help out, but it is most affected by his standpoint with regard to the future and how he is aligned to it. A large successful farm is one which has taken on short term risks with the expectation of long term success.

Farming with animals

Finally, I would like to ground this discussion of risk and following, which is rather abstract, with the animals that the farmers spend so much of their time with; the cows are not passive pawns on the chessboard of the land, after all, but creatures with agency and personality. Most farmers I have met positively *like* the animals; I have been told many tales of their intelligence and character. Cows are individuals, with their own foibles: some are more intelligent than others and can instigate 'break-outs', others hold a grudge and will deliver a sly kick to an unsuspecting farmer. Sheep do not inspire such affection, being seen to be more troublesome than rewarding: they easily lose their ear tags, which can result in a spot fine, and are more difficult to manage. The cows in a farmer's field, by contrast, are a visual display of his competence as a farmer; after a little while I developed an eye for the most obvious features. I remember seeing odd looking cows in a field one day; I was told that these were sunburned. The farmer had a poor reputation and it turned out that the condition of his cattle had been duly noted by all his neighbours. The movements of the cattle between the various fields are also visible. It is not unusual to get stuck behind a herd as it is walked down the road from one field to another and this constant shuffling of animals between fields is necessary to allow the pasture in a field to recover. When I ask farmers how they know when to move their animals they often smile. At one level, they keep an eye on the grass - if it gets too yellow then they know to shift the animals. This is another visible sign of the quality of a farmer's stewardship; the exact point when the farmer chooses to move his animals is debated: some say that the animals should be moved before the grass turns yellow since this will affect the condition of the animals and they will lose a few pounds in weight. Others try to extract all they can from a field before they take the animals to fresh grass. In any case, the cattle will tell the farmer if he leaves them there too long. They will crowd the gate every time the farmer, and even strangers, come near and let out loud bellows if they feel they are being cheated.

The cows are proxies for the intentions of the farmer; they embody and record his decisions, and this record may be read by anyone who has the interest or skill to look at them in the right way.

Success and Failure/Bigger and Smaller on Westray

Euchre is a game of chance and in order to play the participants must take account of the degrees of *risk* which are incumbent on their decisions, and incorporate them into their decision making. Risk, in euchre, is managed in a certain way. In farming, these decisions have important consequences for the long-term success of a farm. On Westray, one could be forgiven for assuming that nothing much changes, that people farm in much the same way as they ever did. It is, after all, one small remote island in an obscure Northern archipelago, not the kind of place where one might expect much by way of innovation or change. Westray, however, is a place where quite bold decisions are occasionally made. The impact of these decisions can be read in the architecture of the farms and in the land holdings which accompany a farm. In particular, some farms can be seen to be growing while others stay the same size or are broken up. This process is the result of risk management but is predicated on a different timescale from that associated with, say, herd management. I see an echo here of the contrast between the individual games of euchre and the larger round of games which comprise an evening of euchre on Westray.

It is interesting to compare the larger farms with the smaller ones, and there is a small group of farms on Westray which are slowly expanding. The process is slow and not always noticeable, given that from the outside all that is visible is a different herd of cows in a field. It is not always possible to pin down why one farm is expanding while another is static. The larger farms (say 75+ animals) have become large by concentrating solely on beef cattle. They manage more livestock and need more land to feed this livestock. Land is necessary not only as grazing but also to grow grass and grain for silage, which is used for winter feed. It is the amount of land which a farm manages, and its quality, which determine the fate of a farm. If a farmer wishes to expand his herd he must eventually find more land. Land is sometimes acquired by purchase, however it is most often rented. There are a small number of landowners who for one reason or another are prepared to rent their land, for example, as mentioned above, they may have their quota but do not wish to actively farm the land, or because they do not live on the island but have inherited land there or they have moved on to other sources of income such as fishing, or again they simply have too much land to cope with. One man inherited a vast estate which had been poorly managed for several years and has been able to deal with only so much, renting the rest. Most farms reach a stage where they can no longer acquire land adjacent to them. They then begin renting or buying plots which are further and further out. These more distant fields are mostly used for silage – cattle are often herded on the public roads and it can be time consuming and awkward to move them too far from their home farm. The farmers like to keep an eye on their beasts and it is easier to do this if they are close at hand.

One advantage of increased size is the ability for the farm to carry more people. Modern farms are highly mechanised, intensive operations which require far fewer people than in the past (one reason for a drop in the population over the last 50 years). It is quite possible for one individual to maintain a farm, yet there are times when it is very difficult to do this without help. If livestock need to be moved very far, especially by road, then several people are needed. The other time when help is needed is in the case of illness. If a farm grows then it also acquires a level of redundancy; it is much easier to cope with the less routine incidents such as when someone is ill, or when animals must be moved. There are economies of scale and the larger farms are better off financially. These outfits are the ones which invest in innovative technologies such as slatted barns and biodigesters.

It is sometimes difficult to give a single reason why one farm might grow while others stay at the same size. At one level this appears to be a result of personality - one farmer I know, who owns a small farm, still grows bere barley as feed. This is a very old variety and no longer commercially grown on any scale. This farmer not only grows it but threshes it for seed for the next year's harvest – its rarity means that it is difficult and expensive to source seed. When I have asked him about this he smiles and points out that it is ideally suited to an Orkney climate and has in fact been bred over hundreds if not thousands of years just for the type of rough weather which is usual in the Northern Isles. It is interesting that no other farmer on Westray grows this and I could put this down to personality.

When I probed deeper, however, it became clear that this was not the whole story. There is a definite element of conservatism, shown by the use of bere barley. This farm was also one which chose not to invest in a slatted barn during the 1970's and at first glance there are few concessions to modernity. The house the farmer lives in has however been thoroughly modernised, is extremely warm and comfortable and he owns up to date farm vehicles. The farm courtyard has not been altered since it was first erected in the 1880's and is in serious need of repair, however there is a brand new barn building tucked away to one side. I would rather see the strategy here as one of 'if it ain't broke don't fix it', and it is one which has served this farmer well. The machine he used to thresh the barley was very old, reputedly pre-war and the first of its kind on the island – a piece of equipment which was once cutting edge.

One other engine for change on farms is the presence of children since farms are still mostly passed on from one generation to the next. The children begin to help with farm work as they grow older and are often seen getting rides in their father's tractor. If the children are interested in working on the farm then it immediately becomes possible to consider buying or renting more land and keeping more cattle. At very busy times of the year, for example when the silage is being harvested, then one sees a constant stream of vehicles on the roads carrying the cut grass back to the farm and several people are needed to operate the machinery for short times.

The path which a farm follows appears to have little to do with seemingly intractable factors such as personality or the number of offspring. It is more that there are choices to be made and these are concerned with risk: the level one is comfortable with and how one manages that risk. All options have a certain risk level attached but one can choose to manipulate the risk, to place it in a sphere where one feels better able to cope with it. There are models of risk in Westray from which one can choose. One can choose to be more daring, to invest in equipment, land, farm buildings and livestock or one can be more risk averse – keep things as they are, adapt only as absolutely necessary. Each farm is faced with many choices as to how they spread their risk and either strategy is acceptable on the island, as long as one does it well. But the farms that do succeed do so because they are managed in an extremely hard-headed business-minded fashion. By this I mean that the larger farms are more successful because they are less risk averse in the short term. They have chosen to become more focussed on one element, beef cattle, almost to the exclusion of any others. The smaller farms have taken a more complicated path – on the one hand they might be seen as more risk averse because they have not borrowed heavily to invest in equipment or land, yet theirs is ultimately the more risky venture – there is less slack in the system here and a small farm can be hit hard by a drop in prices or a change in regulations or illness.

I have been told that most of the farmers on Westray have optimised their farms, so that they do things to the highest standard and achieve the greatest yield for the lowest input, taking into consideration the carrying capacity of the land. They do this on an individual scale, however, rather than at the 'agribusiness' level and so it is each and every farmer's choices which are important.

Back to the Euchre: Following not Leading

For all that the farmers try to control their destiny through decisions such as choosing to spread the sale of their animals over weeks or months, or expanding the herd through land acquisition, there is a side to Westray life which is more to do with following than leading. It is in the sense of following, I would argue, that their farming emerges, just as the play emerges through following the rules of the game. The farmers are after all caught in their rules and regulations and must follow these if they are to *farm* at all. The difference is that the rules a farmer must follow are imposed upon him, they are *regulations.* The rules of euchre are freely agreed upon and the players may walk away at any point. In the end, however, the farmers follow the 'kye' much as the card player does the cards.

In reality there are very few decisions to be made in a game of euchre. If one is good, or bold, one can follow a strategy which will result in greater dividends. It is however perfectly possible to play the game by taking only a few, controlled, risks and to gain a perfectly respectable score by doing so, even if one is unlikely to excel. One can then wait until opportunities present themselves which have no risk attached — sometimes a hand is so good that one simply cannot lose; sometimes it is so bad, or one's opponents so good, that winning is impossible.

Cognition, Cards and Cows

'In general evolved creatures will neither store nor process information in costly ways when they can use the structure of the environment and their operations upon it as a convenient stand-in for the information-processing operations concerned. That is, know only as much as you need to know to get the job done.' (Clark 1989, 64)

Euchre is an example of this type of 'scaffolded' cognition (Clark 1998). The cards hold certain types of information 'out there' in the world where they are most useful. They are useful because others need to see them and to have access to the information. Each card has physical properties — the thickness of the card, its shape and dimensions; its weight and so on. They are light and flexible and make use of designs which are common enough to be utterly familiar to every player. They are mundane and fade into the background, evoking no comment from their users, except when there is something wrong with them. For example, a pack might be slightly tired or sticky from use and then a player might remark on this, especially the older players. Their materiality never becomes invisible, however, but remains a key element in the game since the function of the cards is to carry information, in their own particular way. For the game to work, the information must be portable and it must be presented in such a way that a player may conceal it from others. The ten of hearts, then, can be moved around in one's hand, placed next to others of the same suit and then played at an opportune moment.

The pack of cards encodes a set of relationships which is complete in that it needs no other information to function and does not refer to cards which are not present. The cards carry letters and numbers yet there is no grammar to a pack of cards and the letters and numbers could be replaced with abstract symbols. The cards also carry symbols, which cannot be separated from the card. It is the whole card which is the king of hearts, not the picture of the king. The symbols are arbitrary; all that is truly essential is the relationship between each of the cards. Thus in most games a king is better than a 9, which is better than an 8 and so on. It is also implicated in a set of relationships with other cards and also with the players; it has become part of a human world. One could argue that each card is comparable to a word and that the cards can be manipulated to form strings of meaning. A card, however, does not stand for anything but itself. It is both signifier and signified; it is simply a thing, an object. It is an object which behaves unpredictably, much in the same way as a dice does, when rolled. When the cards are shuffled, or in another player's hand it is difficult to say where a particular card is; various cards will emerge at unexpected points in a game; all a player can do is follow the cards as they are played and try to predict where the missing ones are.

The cards act as proxies for the intentions of the players. They are a record of past moves and are often consulted as such by the players; for example some will check the cards in play on the table before playing their own card: they can work out who played which card, as long as they are in the right order. When the players play their cards their intentions are not so much *represented* by the cards as *borne out* by them. Thus when I play the king of clubs, I am not using it to stand for something else. I am not using the cards to represent some mental game played in my head. I cannot, because the game is communal and is being played on the table before me. The cards, rather, are extensions of my will. They stand in for me, indicate to the others how I have reacted to the previous play. The cards act like a set of directions which can be followed in sequence. If a player plays the 9 of clubs then the logical step for the next player is the 10 or a trump card. At each point the player can have a choice but for the most part only one response is correct.

This is what the players on Westray mean when they say they just 'follow the cards'. The cards are used to guide the play, which is probably why everyone is quite relaxed. Farming decisions can likewise be 'scaffolded'. The cattle, for example, can themselves tell the farmers when they must be brought in for the winter or moved to another field. Are the cattle and the farmer in some kind of cognitive symbiosis?

The scaffolding here involves objects, and more than one person, and is somewhat similar to Hutchins' (1995) account of distributed cognition. It is also, following Donald (1991), a form of external symbolic storage; and can even be understood, in the terms of Clark and Chalmers (2010), as the workings of an extended mind, or minds, since it is a shared activity. The cards are used in such a way that they come to determine actions; they help the player, they are pointers to action and can be used as such. On the one hand they are proxies which carry the intention of the players; on the other hand they determine the actions of the players.

There is also a link between proxy actions and mimicry. The players' intentions are extended towards the cards, which in turn are taken as proxies. It is not so much that you want to do something as that you want the cards to do it for you and so the cards carry the intentions of the players. It is a form of mimicry but at a distance and mediated by objects. The cards are a kind of mask, then: they mediate the intentions of the player while at the same time helping the player to disguise his or her intentions. A cognitive sleight of hand transfers the player's opponents' attention away from him or her towards the cards, or chess pieces.

These objects in turn scaffold thought and support further actions and there is a way in which the game influences the progress and timing of cognition. The rules, the ways in which the players must allow their thoughts and actions to take place in step with the game, all combine with the result that thought and action are effectively *ratcheted* forwards along a path.

Following Rules, Taking Directions.

What *is* a card game like euchre? It is definitely a form of play, but to analyse it purely as play risks getting tangled in definitions. If there is a problem with play theory, as we have already seen in Chapter 1, it is the acknowledged vagueness of the subject, which is probably why so much ink has been spilled in attempts to define it (e.g. Huizinga 1950, Spariousou 1989, Sutton Smith 1997, Caillois 2001, Hendry & Raveri 2002 etc.), and why so many attitudes to play exist. There is Freud's theory of play as something used by adults to 'master a chaotic world' and Piaget's theory of play as something used by children to 'accommodate' the world (1962); Huizinga would see it as the root of all 'culture' while Geertz treated it as an irrelevant side show (1993). One other problem is that much of play theory rests on a central tenet, first put forward by Huizinga 70 years ago, that play is something which is formally set apart (Huizinga 1950); if it is truly set apart it becomes difficult to set play in context (Piaget 1962). At the same time there have been many attempts to use play as a metaphor for society; this is, after all, a 're-creation' of the world, a playful inversion of normality (Muir 1997, 85-116).

When Geertz discussed cock fighting in Bali (Geertz 1993) he declared that his participation in this play event had resulted in his and his wife's acceptance by the local community, through the mediation of a sudden police raid. When the police arrived he acted instinctively and fled in panic with the natives. This is an example of how participation in play can lead to integration within a wider community. Riches (1975) argued that the qualities of a game were suited to the place and particular qualities of a given situation within which it was nested. In that case, poker was played by the men while out hunting, while more sedate card games were played by the women and children in the settlement. Both cases are interesting because they point towards the way play is suited to its environment, and indicate that play is less bounded, less set apart than some have assumed (Huizinga 1950, Murray 1952, Geertz 1993). Moreover they are not alone, since there have been many other attempts to demonstrate how play is adapted to suit particular places or situations. Euchre, I would argue, also displays these qualities and in this case, the game is inclusive and adapted to life in a small island community. The argument is easily made, however — all activities in a given community must be adaptive to a certain extent if there is not to be a clash between activity and community. It would obviously be ridiculous to expect games requiring massive infrastructure, complex logistics and large audiences to be adopted somewhere such as Westray.

Euchre has much in common with chess. For example, both are played in social situations. Both co-opt objects into the play and both are games of strategy (see Huizinga 1950, Murray 1952 and Caillois 2001) but in the case of euchre, however, I found that in many games I could not effectively implement a strategy at all and had very little choice over what card I played. This happens in chess also, of course, where a good player can take control of the board, leaving the opponent with few worthwhile choices, however chance is not implicated here. In euchre a player could be dealt such a good hand that it simply did not matter what card I played, so long as they made no obvious mistake. Sometimes my choice was governed entirely by the cards which others played. Another instance where strategy failed was when play was fast and there were too many decisions with equal or near equal weighting — I very often just played the first card that came to hand, sometimes with dreadful consequences. A few players consistently make high scores, however, which suggests that successful strategies do exist. But whenever I asked a player about their method, I was always told that they 'just followed the cards.'

Euchre, in common with most games, has a well-defined set of rules which collectively form a *structure*. The rules shape the activity and give it a form. They serve to distinguish this game from all the others with different rules; they govern the behaviour of the players. At the same time the choices made by the players and their behaviour during play contribute to and influence the structure. The structure is, then reflexive; it is also simple and robust, it withstands the occasional infraction and is readily understood by all participants. The structure is inclusive and is known to all.

The structure is prominent and it provides a backdrop or stage against which the action occurs. But it is also woven into the fabric of the game. The rules do not all come into force at the same time, it is more a case of 'if this then do that…or if that then this'. The cards physically embody some of the rules and they will be encountered as one works one's way through the game. The rules, then, are like way-stations in the game, close enough to control the outline yet far enough apart to permit process to emerge. As a player plays he navigates the rules, he follows them one to another. The rules, then, do not so much impose boundaries which divide the game into manageable sections, as lay down pathways or pointers which control and direct flow (Olwig 2008, 88) in a form of process.

The structure rests on the process, and the structure emerges more or less as the game unfolds. The play is ultimately defined by the actions of the players and not by the presence of the rules. If the players stop playing the structure 'collapses' and all that is left is a list of rules and a pack of cards. A comparison might be with music and the performance of a musician. The musician has his sheet music, covered in musical notation. This notation is surely comparable to the rules of a game; it serves to control the behaviour of the player and to set one particular piece of music apart from any other. The musician works his way through the notes, encountering new ones and new combinations as he goes, yet the music is there in the performance, not in the notation. If one wished to understand play or music, one would want to play a game or hear the score as it is performed.

At the same time as I can see the game as actively shaped by the participants through their decision making, it is just as interesting and rewarding to examine the way they simply follow the rules. Decision-making is necessary; however there are only a small number of occasions when these decisions are difficult or particularly crucial, for example the choice of trump following dealing. Otherwise, the choices, such as which card to play, are usually simple: for the most part a player will respond to previous decisions from a small repertoire: one card from a choice of at most five in any situation. There are external factors to be taken into account, such as one's partner, but in effect, once the deck has been shuffled and trump 'made' the game will play itself out in a fairly predictable way, so long as the players are of an average standard. Mistakes do of course occur and a bad decision can be made at any time but this is not to say that the Westray euchre players are not skilled; skill is essential to play the game at their level.

If the players follow the cards the lack of complex decision making allows for speed to be built up and a certain tempo to be achieved. This tempo is part of the play and it is noticeable when it breaks down, for instance when a player takes too long to play. Players in Westray are usually extremely patient but just now and then there would come the combination of a poor or slow player with another player who was more voluble. Then there would be a couple of comments, though nearly always and deliberately good natured.

For the farmer (and the fisherman), who seems to be surrounded by rules and regulations, he too is part of a structure which controls his actions. If he chooses not to follow the rules then he will be forced to stop farming. A farmer can only farm so long as he follows these rules, yet the farmers I spoke to do not define themselves by them. Farming exists separately from these rules and the farmer lives his life in the way he approaches them, in his unique interaction with them and in the run-up to the next encounter with a rule.

Much of this chapter has taken euchre, and farming, on Westray, as activities where rules are important, yet the relationship with the rules is not straightforward. The rules lead; the euchre player, the farmer, follows. There is no need to see the rules as boundaries since much of what goes on does so in the gaps between the rules. The rules indicate directions of travel, yet the method of arrival can be varied and interesting.

There are many other activities which are also hedged around with rules, for example fishing, but I chose farming as representative of Westray and as an interesting point of comparison. This chapter related my experience of euchre, and found many of the same themes which I had seen in chess, though in a different context. In the next section I turn to the archaeology and explore the potential of this resource for the study of play.

Chapter 4

Counters

Introduction

With this chapter I now turn to the archaeology of play and here I introduce one small data set. This is a type of gaming piece — counters — for which there is a limited amount of information and my response here has been to turn towards the concept of bricolage since I have found it a helpful way to understand how these objects can interact.

The counters I discuss here were recovered from contexts which can be generally dated to the first few centuries AD. There are only a few objects known from earlier periods which may relate to play. Childe, for example, categorised two published 'cubical blocks of ivory' from Skara Brae (Childe 1931: 154) as dice, and a further, unpublished, bone object also from Skara Brae (held by Tankerness House Museum) has also been interpreted as a gaming piece. All these pieces are, however, more likely to represent bead making debris or bead blanks (unfinished beads, see Foxon 1985). There is little evidence for play from the Bronze Age; however one exception may be the large group of 59+ sheep astragali found at Bayanne, in Shetland (Moore and Wilson 2014). These bones could represent no more than a hoard of bones curated for some practical, everyday function such as hide preparation but they are puzzling; moreover astragali are well known from classical contexts as a form of dice or random number generator often associated with divination or 'astragalomancy', based on the property that the bones will naturally and unpredictably come to rest on one of four sides if thrown. However, even the few very large scale excavations of Bronze Age settlement sites, for example the Lairg project (McCullagh and Tipping 1998) or Links of Noltland (Moore and Wilson 2006-2013, 2011a), or Corrstown (admittedly in Northern Ireland, but close enough to be relevant: see Ginn & Rathbone 2012), have yielded no material culture one could readily associate with play. This picture is the same for Bronze Age burials. The artefact-rich inhumations associated with the Beaker period and the early 2 millennium urn burials generally give way to simple cist burials (although see recent excavations at Links of Noltland for a slightly different sequence) yet do not contain gaming pieces. As we move on to the early Iron Age, from c.800BC (see Ritchie & Ritchie 1991, Edwards & Ralston 2003) there may be fewer excavated sites, but we still do not find gaming pieces. It is only when we come to the late Iron Age (LIA), from around the second or third century AD, that the picture begins to change.

My conclusion is that the earliest good evidence for board games in Scotland appears with counters. These small objects do not seem to be tools, or be decorative, or to be involved with subsistence activities. Fortunately, they appear at a time when Roman incursions into the south of Scotland brought other board games which used counters and for which there is better literary evidence (see Hall 2007, Hall forthcoming). By comparison with this corpus it seems certain that the counters I discuss here were in fact gaming pieces and it is likely also that the games being played in *Atlantic Scotland* at this time derive from contact with the Roman world and that variants on some of the same games were played.

If it is difficult to locate play in archaeological contexts in Scotland prior to the 1 millennium AD, this must reflect a combination of the types of play taking place, the nature of the evidence and my own criteria. I do not accept that play was not taking place: play is a fundamental human (mammalian, even, see Sutton-Smith 1998) activity. Either the evidence does not survive, or the types of play taking place did not leave the kind of evidence I could identify.

It is interesting that counters continue to be used, even following the introduction of more complex games such as Tafl later in the 1 millennium AD. They have never been discussed in detail and remain little more than a footnote in most excavation reports,

Figure 2. Selection of counters from Clickhimin broch, Shetland (Jenny Murray).

even where they are recognised as a category (Hall 2008, Sharples 1998, Moore & Wilson 2014). They are, however, an interesting example of play and of material culture since a consideration of counters must entail an exploration of sets; how things are brought together to form groups which have dynamic interrelationships and how the presence of the set, or group, alters our understanding of the lone thing.

My study area here is Shetland during the first few centuries of the 1 millennium AD, where two sites yielded unusually large numbers of gaming pieces, Clickhimin (Hamilton 1968) and Upper Scalloway Broch (Sharples 1998), and the finds from here have formed the basis for my discussion (see figure 2).

Sets

Counters are small, unassuming objects, simple discs of stone (sometimes polished), pottery, bone or glass. Their small size (usually less than 5cm in diameter) and subtle modifications means that they do not always stand out as finds, during excavation, and as a consequence they can be very easily overlooked, stone counters can be particularly difficult to spot. They are, however, a persistent element of finds assemblages from this period onwards and are worthy of study, even if it may be difficult to tease out much information.

A counter may seem to be rather undistinguished, or bland, however this is related to their purpose, and is in any case an attribute which is most obvious when they are considered singly, separated from their 'pack'. Games which use counters are most often concerned with in strategic, rather than tactical, aims (Murray 1952). A modern example of a game which uses counters is 'Go', or the pawns in chess could be considered as counters – similar pieces of small individual worth which nevertheless have an important role in the larger game. Counters look small and insignificant but can do important things. The most obvious way in which they achieve this is by acting in concert with other counters and this is done in the form of *sets* of pieces.

Objects, artefacts, are very often discussed together in terms of archaeological assemblages (Joyce & Pollard 2010) but it is unusual to analyse objects in terms of sets and I will distinguish sets from assemblages here on the basis that a set of objects has more active relationships. An assemblage, particularly in the archaeological sense, is too often a static group of things. Childe (1925, 1935) was perhaps one of the first to make use of the concept in archaeology, but he did so out of a desire to use assemblages of objects to identify cultures rather than out of an interest in the relationships between objects and people - there is no sense that objects can influence one another, that their movement and the movement of people around them changes how they are perceived, how people think and act in their vicinity. Perhaps the closest archaeology comes to this is with the application of the concept of 'structured deposition' to certain assemblages (Hill 1995, Joyce & Pollard 2010). Recent work at Links of Noltland, in Orkney has encountered structured deposition; there it is interpreted in terms of 'composition' (Moore & Wilson 2011a).

A set of counters, or gaming pieces, is a collection of objects brought together for a purpose. There are many types of composite objects where different things are joined together: an arrow, or a plough, for example. The arrow might comprise a wooden shaft, a flint arrowhead and feather flights. Glue and twine might be used to join the various pieces together. A standard archaeological analysis might follow the *chaine operatoire* – the sequence of events necessary in order to bring about the final finished product, and might consider the social implications of, for example, access to flint sources or choice of wood, but would not consider the group as a set. A set, I believe, is a looser, but more *dynamic*, arrangement of objects, one where the individual components are allowed the freedom to move and to influence the others. Many composite objects could probably be understood better in terms of the set: in the case of the arrow, the feathers might be moved or the arrowhead replaced. New ways of using the arrow might be discovered as the arrow's flight characteristics are altered and its appearance will change as new parts are added.

Bricolage

I think that one way of appreciating how sets of things, such as counters, work is to begin with a consideration of *bricolage*, a concept which was first brought to anthropology by Lévi-Strauss (1966). I do not want to import Lévi-Strauss's theory wholesale here because there are problems with his use of bricolage, which I will describe below. I will, however, begin with his approach since it has been influential, and has a place in the history of theory.

Bricolage is useful because it can help us understand how games make use of sets. In a game, different objects are brought together, for example on the gaming board. There is a way in which the objects on each side act together as one, and there is also a way in which these disparate things remain discrete. Individual gaming pieces flip between these aspects as the game progresses and are often removed entirely when the opposing side *isolates* and captures them. It is often necessary for a player to break their opponents' pieces out of that set in order to perform the capture. Bricolage allows for an understanding of objects as things which act together but which need not lose their identity in the process. Iron Age counters were likewise used together, yet I would argue that they did not entirely lose their individual identities. This might have been expressed in the small variations in colour or pattern visible on their surfaces, or their textures, which would be known to their owners, who might have played with some gaming pieces tens or hundreds of times before they were lost or abandoned. Some counters have been refashioned from older artefacts, for example pottery, and it is clear that these, at least, possess histories, biographies. The game, however, has brought the diverse counters together to form something new, at the same time it does not entirely subsume them in this new thing, the set. I argue that this is a form of bricolage, and a useful way of understanding some forms of play.

I should say here that since I have been led towards bricolage by sets *my* use of the concept begins with things, the material world, whereas Lévi-Strauss was more concerned with symbolic thought. Also, I go on to more modern approaches and consider bricolage in art terms, which I believe is relevant.

Lévi-Strauss applied bricolage to his theory of 'mythical thought' (1966, 16-18, 30). He argued that the concept was useful in addressing a particular way of ordering the world:

> 'The characteristic feature of mythical thought is that it expresses itself by means of a heterogeneous repertoire which, even if extensive, is nevertheless limited. It has to use this repertoire, however, whatever the task in hand because it has nothing else at its disposal. Mythical thought is therefore a kind of intellectual 'bricolage'...' (1966, 17).

Lévi-Strauss discussed the meaning of the word: bricolage, in the original French, was used to describe a certain unexpected or unpredictable quality to an event, such as a horse swerving, a dog straying, or a ball rebounding (1966, 16). The 'bricoleur' was a 'handyman' (as opposed to an 'engineer'), someone who makes do with the materials to hand. Lévi-Strauss borrowed the term to imply two things: firstly, the use of pre-existing things in the creation of something new and, secondly, the unpredictable nature, or outcome, of the new construction. Finally, of course, he took a word or concept most often applied to practical things and used it to describe an abstract theory of the mind and in doing so wished to draw a distinction between different kinds of thought: the handyman bricoleur versus the engineer/scientist. The handyman is limited by his pre-existing repertoire of materials and tools. The engineer is aware of his repertoire but never limited by it; he is always free to plan his project beforehand and works in terms of concepts. The handyman must find his way to the solution by working through the options, eventually arriving at an essentially unexpected destination; he works in terms of the concrete, of signs. The engineer keeps the destination in mind and will look beyond his repertoire to achieve it. The bricoleur's engagement with the world is, then, for Lévi-Strauss characterised in terms of the use of pre-existing concepts and their adaptation to new purposes, but he is *constrained* by his 'mind-set'. It seems clear that for Lévi-Strauss the bricoleur must be *unable* to look beyond these pre-existing concepts, whatever they are.

Lévi-Strauss sought to present bricolage as fundamental, however in doing so he created a contradiction, 'inadvertently shifting levels from the mind to the agent whose mind it is' (*pers. Comm.* Ingold) since the implication is that the engineer is also a bricoleur but at a deeper level, somehow. Lévi-Strauss sought to draw a line between bricoleur and engineer in terms of a distinction between improvisation and innovation, and this distinction is still of interest, if we leave behind the bricoleur vs. engineer 'dead end'. The bricoleur works with the materials to hand; he improvises. The engineer seeks novel solutions; he looks beyond his surroundings and innovates. Improvisation is process-led; the goal, if it exists, is found by exploring the possibilities (or affordances, Gibson 1979) of the environment and adapting them to new purposes. Bricolage, then, leads towards a consideration of the nature of creativity.

Derrida (1970) took the concept of bricolage (from Lévi-Strauss) and used it to describe a system where there is no 'centre', where meaning can be arbitrary and self-referential. This system is 'playful', to use the word in Derrida's sense: it has give and take; it does not have 'truth value' but only a central idea which, in effect, keeps the whole together and lends it shape. We can see, here, a use for play which is close to the ludic (Huizinga 1950, 27): an activity or system such as a game has its own logic, its own internal rules. The bricoleur, for Derrida, works within a system which may be flawed but does not attempt to look outside it to find meaning; instead, he works with what he has and creates new meanings through the fresh juxtaposition of the pre-existing. The relationships between the elements within the system are enough to create meaning. Derrida, like Lévi-Strauss, also draws a distinction between bricoleur and 'engineer'; here the engineer is one who deals in systems without play, ones which are anchored by external references. Since the engineer looks beyond the system for meaning he is not constrained by it.

Derrida's use of 'play' to describe bricolage is interesting. His definition of bricolage would also be acceptable as a way to describe play and is very similar to Huizinga's classic definition. Here, Derrida characterises bricolage as a system which need not be grounded but has its own internal logic. It is the relationships between the elements within the system which are important. If there is one difference here between play and bricolage it would be in the area of free choice. For Huizinga, one of the key attributes of play is the ability of the participants to take part at will (Huizinga 1950, 10). For Derrida, and Lévi-Strauss, the bricoleur has no option but to *be* a bricoleur. At the same time, and taking account of commentators such as Wynn, who attest that we are all bricoleurs, that the distinction between engineer and bricoleur is a false one, the possibility emerges of an understanding of these systems in terms of play. To put it another way, if we engage with the world in terms of a kind of bricolage ('every discourse is bricoleur' (Derrida 1970)), and if bricolage can be understood as play, should we not accept that our engagement with the world is fundamentally ludic, or play-full?

Wynn has applied the concept of bricolage at a very practical level, to problem solving and tool use. Wynn cites blacksmithing (following Keller and Keller 1991, see Wynn 1994, 149) as his example, the 'constellations of conceptual units' which the craftsman blacksmith employs (Lévi-Strauss elides craftsman with 'engineer', see 1966, 17-20) are his repertoire that is continually, repeatedly, employed in the fashioning of new items. Wynn sees the distinction between handy man bricoleur and 'engineer', which forms the core of Lévi-Strauss's argument, as false. If there is such a thing as 'mythical thought' it is employed by craftsman and bricoleur alike, or, to put it another way, each of us is a bricoleur.

In their discussion of creativity and improvisation, Ingold and Hallam (2007) identified two kinds of creativity: 'kaleidoscopic', which corresponds to bricolage, and 'concrescence' (see also Ingold 2007 and Sansi 2015, 127). They favour the latter kind and point towards creativity as inherent in improvisation, '...people have to work it out as they go along. In a word, they have to *improvise*.' (Ingold & Hallam 2007, 1, emphasis in original) and situate this form of creativity as 'part of a process of growth, of bringing into being or becoming' (pers. comm. Ingold, following Bergson 1911 and Whitehead 1929, see Ingold 2007a, 47). Lévi-Strauss never made it clear how the bricoleur improvises or the nature of his source material, except that he works with 'signs' (1966, 20). For Ingold and Hallam our lives are improvised: we are not bound by *scripts* but 'responsive to continually changing environmental conditions' (2007, 12), our responses are of necessity honed through long practice and become skilled engagements with the world at hand. They point out that:

> '...improvisation... is inherently temporal. This is a time, however, that is not marked out by the oscillations of a perfectly repeating system such as a clock or metronome or by the revolutions of the planets, but one that is lived and felt in the pulsating rhythms of life itself. Though it is a linear time, its linearity is of a particular kind. It is not the kind of line that goes from point to point, connecting up a succession of present instants arrayed diachronically as locations in space might be arrayed synchronically. It is rather a line that grows, issuing forth from its advancing tip rather like a root or creeper probes the earth.' (Ingold and Hallam 2007: 10-11).

Ingold and Hallam's discussion of improvisation and time brings together some of the concepts under discussion here. In the Kellers' blacksmithing (Keller and Keller 1991), for example, the 'constellations of conceptual units' endlessly repeated to form new items is an instance of improvisation. No two of these conceptual units can ever be exactly the same and so their repetition becomes rhythmic rather than metronomic (Ingold and Hallam 2007: 10), their creativity is undiminished by repetition since it is always anchored in temporality and is always a fresh attempt to grapple with changing circumstances. The blacksmith edges towards the finished object by using all he (or she) has learnt, working constantly with the changing circumstances and materials as they are presented to him.

It is within the tightly controlled framework of the game that players must improvise, and it is within this framework that creativity emerges, as improvisation, which is structured according to the resources available to it. Just as improvisation is temporal (Ingold and Hallam 2007), so is play. The game advances in linear fashion, each step must be preceded by a previous one and followed by another until the game ends. Play makes time concrete and visible and open to manipulation. Players can move quickly to rush and confuse their opponent or slowly to frustrate. Play is improvisation. It does not depend on rules or scripts but works around them, responding not to the rules but to the changing, unpredictable actions of another. Huizinga argued that play stands outside of time: for him it is a-temporal and bounded by the rules; play as improvisation is the opposite, it creates time, is bound up with and reacts to the environment.

Neither Lévi-Strauss nor Derrida seem to have been unduly concerned with the creativity of bricolage. Judging from the tone of Lévi-Strauss's comments, one of the important distinctions between the bricoleur and the engineer is the limited nature of bricolage; it is not creative, for Lévi-Strauss, because it deals only with a given vocabulary. As Ingold and Hallam point out, however, a limited vocabulary is *inevitably* creative. Derrida sought to cut bricolage free of external references, to make his system self-referential.

More recently, Roger Sansi's discussion of bricolage (Sansi 2015) contrasted Ingold with Lévi-Strauss in terms of creativity. Bricolage is a way of interacting with the world. For Sansi, Lévi-Strauss's notion of Bricolage is a 'rearrangement of pre-existing forms through a punctual event of encounter – a 'revelation,' as it were. As opposed to this, Ingold's notion of 'concrescence' insists on the continuous process of unfolding of 'life', of forms, rather than punctual events' (Sansi 2015, 127).

If counters can be said to encapsulate bricolage, how does creativity fit into the discussion? Creativity is necessary to make sense of the disparate elements. The player must make the best of the circumstances which are presented to him or her on the board and, much like the blacksmith, edges his way forwards through the game. Always, he works with a limited repertoire of pieces set against a tightly defined 'landscape' – the board – but he must do his best to find new combinations of movement which will confound the opponent.

Art Bricolage

Bricolage is also a form of art, if not an art movement in its own right, and a brief consideration of art and bricolage is relevant here because it usefully highlights a slightly different aspect of bricolage, allowing for a different appreciation of the archaeological evidence. Colin Renfrew has discussed the relationship between art and archaeology (Renfrew 2003) and seeks to show the similarities between artist and archaeologist by examining the ways they work with their respective subjects. For Renfrew, 'art can be the expression in the material world of a concept' (2003: 99) but he does not seek to show how art may cast light on topics which are relevant to archaeology (and anthropology), for example, the manipulation of objects to create different understandings or appreciations of the world.

Found Objects

In art terms, bricolage describes an artwork where various different objects are brought together to form a new whole. The pre-existing objects are often found items - 'readymades' - which can bring their own associations or indeed can be purposely void of association or even interest. Duchamp, for example, when he chose a readymade, looked for an object which '...wouldn't attract me, either by its beauty or by its ugliness...' (1966: BBC interview with Joan Bakewell). If an object began to interest him then he would discard it immediately. Joseph Beuys, by contrast, used things which had some personal or wider social significance. Duchamp and Beuys, and artists like them, may make us reconsider what art is but they do this through objects, by taking the pre-existing and placing it in a new context. Duchamp's 'fountain', the urinal entered for the 1917 Independents exhibition (and rejected), or his 'shadows of readymades' (1918), or even 'Bottle Rack' (1913), delight in transforming our understanding of everyday objects. Beuys' 'vitrines' such as 'untitled' (1986) or 'model for a felt environment' (1964) took museum display cases and filled them with familiar objects. His sculptures, and his larger installations, or 'environments' (for example 'The Pack', 1969), likewise use 'readymades'.

Duchamp was also a conceptual artist, and improvisatory. His *3 stoppages etalon* ('Three Standard Stoppages') of 1913-1914 was an 'experiment ... to imprison and preserve forms obtained through chance'. (d'Harnoncourt, A & McShine, K eds., *Marcel Duchamp*, exhibition catalogue, Philadelphia Museum of Art, 1973, pp.273-4.). I should also say that I like Duchamp because he gave up art to follow chess, arguing I think (and quite rightly) that chess was much more important.

The Dadaists, like Duchamp, are often associated more with assemblage, yet there is sometimes only a fine difference between bricolage and assemblage: the art assemblage is a juxtaposition of objects which remain essentially unaltered (very similar to a standard archaeological 'assemblage'). Joseph Cornell's Medici Slot Machine boxes are, however, a good example of assemblages which are designed to be manipulated and changed by the visitor. Bricolage incorporates objects, and can change them, and in this process the new artwork allows for a reinterpretation of their constituent materials. The reinterpretation can be startling, amusing or subverting and for this to work, the original objects must still be identifiable in some way. Bricolage art is a creative reordering, a way of challenging accepted norms, a way to bring about a reconsideration of objects with apparently fixed connotations, or, conversely, to view objects which seem to be utterly unremarkable in a new light. Bricolage is conceptual; it expresses an interest in the relationship between ideas and objects; between object and object.

Art bricolage is also temporal. It never loses its connection with the world because the objects never entirely lose their original connotations. The creativity of art bricolage is improvisatory, it is inherent in the artist's engagement with the world around him, his knowledge and attention to the objects surrounding him and their present and potential associations. The juxtapositions which the bricolage brings about are dynamic and surprising.

It is also interesting to compare bricolage with montage, which are very similar. In montage, pre-existing elements are brought together to form a new image in which these elements are subsumed. A common modern example of montage is the computer generated pictures formed by hundreds of very small pictures which can only be seen by very close inspection. With bricolage, the elements are never completely lost, and the strength of the work often relies on the individual elements never entirely losing the connotations of their original function. Montage is also primarily to do with paintings or images whereas bricolage is far more concerned with objects, with things, and is so much more relevant to play and board games.

In the next section I explore some examples of play taken from the archaeological record. I want to look afresh at certain objects which have been recovered from excavations, keeping bricolage and improvisation in mind, and I want to examine them not only as gaming pieces but as objects with associations and histories. The advantage of using archaeology for this kind of study is first and foremost that it is a discipline which routinely deals with objects. Museums are full of objects and archaeologists have evolved many strategies to record, preserve and publish their artefacts. It is possible, therefore, to use archaeological publications to gain access to an extremely wide range of things, together with the various specialist discussions which categorise and measure and place them within the relevant typologies. Archaeologists are also concerned with the provenance or context of objects as well as the taphonomy and formation processes by which objects get to be where they were when found. Chronology, whether the relative kind of pottery seriation or the absolute kind associated with radiocarbon dating, gives these objects relationships, sometimes with one another, sometimes with other elements such as changing architectural styles or geographical areas. Archaeology, then, has much to offer to a study of objects and the converse is also true since it is fair to say that while some elements of the archaeological record, pottery for example, are exhaustively studied, archaeology is not so good at appreciating the dynamic relationships between objects. There are types of activity represented by objects which are routinely ignored or dismissed and the evidence for play is one of these.

Shetland Counters

Shetland has benefitted from several fairly large scale programmes of excavation in recent years, which has resulted in an excellent data set. There are also many older excavations, which even if they were carried out to a lesser standard have at least been published. Two major sites of the prehistoric and early historic periods in Atlantic Scotland, Jarlshof and Clickhimin (Hamilton 1956, 1968), are located here. In addition, the local Sites and Monuments Record (SMR) is well maintained and the islands thus provide a well-defined research area with a good quality data set; their relative isolation is, furthermore, more geographical than cultural and the archaeology of Shetland, particularly from the Iron Age onwards, fits readily with the rest of Atlantic Scotland.

A wide range of gaming equipment has been recovered from Shetland sites of the 1 millennium AD. The material first appears around the 3 century AD, in the form of simple small counters. Taken as a whole, the evidence from Shetland suggests that there was a kind of play 'watershed', when board games were adopted or invented, and that after that point these counters form a recurring element of finds assemblages. The adoption of board games forms a reliable 'horizon' within the archaeological record and the presence of counters also, and more interestingly, marks a change in attitudes towards, or uses of, material culture.

Nearly every site on Shetland which contains deposits dating from the early 1 millennium AD onwards has produced some counters, however two sites stand out in terms of the quantity of material recovered: Clickhimin (Hamilton 1968) and Scalloway (Sharples 1998). Together, these sites have produced probably the largest assemblage of gaming equipment from Atlantic Iron Age Scotland. They also to some degree complement one another and between them have yielded a sequence which begins in the later Bronze Age and runs on to the early medieval period. The interpretation of these two sites is not simple: both are complex multi period settlements and have their own peculiar problems. Clickhimin, for example, was excavated some 60 years ago and although it was excavated to a high level, according to the standards of the day, archaeological techniques and interpretations have since moved on and it would benefit from a full re-evaluation if it is to remain relevant. Scalloway was excavated over late 1989 and spring 1990 to a high standard by a professional team, yet this was a rapid rescue excavation and information was lost due to the actions of developers.

It is interesting to contrast the two excavations, particularly with reference to the archaeological evidence for play. With Scalloway, the post-excavation analysis proceeded smoothly, with the artefacts being divided into the various conventional categories, such as worked bone, coarse stone, metalwork and so on. An unusual feature of the Scalloway publication report is the way in which the categories were then discussed in terms of the processes which gave rise to their formation, for example a range of artefact types might be brought together thematically under vessels (including metal, stone, ceramic). In the case of gaming equipment, counters were identified at an early stage in the process and subsequently analysed and discussed as a group. The objects identified as counters comprised a number of small stone discs and small polished stones. There was no confusion with other similar objects, such as pot lids, since these had been identified and separated out. It was not possible to say how exactly the counters were used since the game was not identified; their identification as gaming pieces rested on the simple fact that no other use could be imagined for them. So, an object might look like a gaming piece, a counter, but if was pierced it would have been classified as a bead; if it was rather large then it might be classified as a pot lid (for a small pot). If it showed signs of use wear then it might have been classed as a tool: a plough pebble perhaps. My point is not that counters were wrongly classified, only that the process by which they were identified was somewhat arbitrary, and would not stand up to close scrutiny; but then, it must be admitted that the processes by which archaeologists categorise and discuss objects are rarely overtly discussed (see Olson 2010 and Conneller 2011). I do not want to labour this point, but it is interesting and pertinent to my overall discussion because it gets at the ambiguity of the evidence for play; it also leads on to Clickhimin and the problems the excavator there had in identifying play at that site.

The evidence for play from Clickhimin seems on the face of it to be as well defined as that from Scalloway and there are sections of the report which deal specifically with counters. When one takes a closer look, however, not all is as it seems. Some eight objects are classed as counters in the published report, yet another 104 small discs are catalogued but not as gaming pieces. Why is this? The small discs are all about the same size – 5cm or less. They are variously termed 'pot-lids', 'discs', 'schist discs' or 'plaques', yet it is clear that they would not fit any of these functions, being too small or fragile, or too finely made (for example, polished) or made of unusual stone. I would say that the true number of counters is closer to 112 or more than ten times the published number. My feeling is that the excavator, John Hamilton, had a very clear idea of what was and wasn't a counter, his definition was very restricted and if an object did not exactly fit this it was assumed to be something else, possibly more utilitarian even if a function could not be defined. At Scalloway, by contrast, there was no fixed expectation of what a gaming piece should look like, and thus a wider range of material was included, allowing for a more rounded appreciation of play at this site.

The counters at both sites did not always occur as isolated objects. They could be found in twos or threes and some contexts and areas had more than others; it is possible to isolate groups of counters by size or location and so to form sets. It is clear, in fact, that these objects were used in sets, and this is how we are brought back to bricolage. The sets juxtapose different stone types, from different sources, as well as a few made of other materials, for example pottery. The material has almost always been altered in some way to create the counter - for example, polished, trimmed, facetted or ground down - yet the parent material always remains apparent and the sets, for all that they share attributes, can at the same time be quite heterogeneous.

When one examines these counters it is possible to say something of where they came from; they have histories. One might have been a beach pebble, another once formed part of a pot. At Clickhimin, several counters were made of garnetiferous schist, a distinctive, shiny, stone found in several places in Shetland (Mykura 1976). Each one is distinctive and not exactly like any other. There is no sense that the counters in a set would have been made at the same time – that, say, twenty similar pieces of pottery or stone were chosen and then shaped until identical. Rather, the sense is that various pieces of stone or pottery were encountered by the would-be player at different times and then kept or curated until enough had been gathered to form a set. At Clickhimin, the site lies on the coast edge, a handy source of stone. Beach pebbles have many uses and are found frequently on archaeological sites in Shetland: the larger ones can make good pounders, or can be reshaped to provide other tools, such as 'flaked stone bars' (agricultural tools) or 'skaill knives' (butchery tools). The beach is a place which routinely offers useful materials, it is a resource, as well as a work place. The small, counter-sized beach stones *afford* a use as gaming pieces (Gibson 1979, Hodder 2012, Knappett 2005), in the sense that their properties allow these qualities to 'come into play' (Hodder 2012;113). All of the stones on a beach must have several affordances: from building materials to weights, tools, decorative objects and even skimmers (Knappett 2005; 58-59). If one 'affordance' is recognised and made use of this does not mean that all others must be lost. In the case of some of the stone gaming pieces there is a sense in which they can 'flip' between gaming piece and beach pebble (in fact many of the Clickhimin examples were excavated from layers deposited on a beach), depending on the context: they have not lost all of the distinctive polish and rounded shape which gives away their source. This illustrates a key property of play; it can be said to exist as a kind of affordance which is present in every object and can be utilised if one so wishes, without necessarily altering the properties of the object or ruling out other affordances.

This 'flip-flopping' between affordances brings me back to bricolage. The beach pebbles, the pot sherds, are the 'readymades' which are brought together to form the new whole, the *set*. Ideally, they should be like Duchamp's readymades: neither so beautiful nor so ugly as to attract too much attention. The set is created by many separate elements, each of which does not entirely lose its previous connotations, its affordances, and in so doing the new whole is composed of different objects, things with their own histories, their own trajectories. This tension is creative and best understood in terms of bricolage. The counters are brought together to form the set and relationships between them are generated and exploited during play.

Returning to the archaeological setting for these counters, it is clear, as mentioned above, that they first appear around the 3 century AD. This point in time is interesting in terms of discussions concerning the Iron Age of Atlantic Scotland. For Foster (Foster 1990, Barrett & Foster 1991) it occupies the transition to LIA1: the decline of the nucleated, hierarchical, broch settlements typified by sites like Gurness (Hedges 1987), Howe (Ballin Smith 1994) Jarlshof (Hamilton 1956) and Clickhimin (Hamilton 1968). Recent excavations at sites like Bayanne (Moore and Wilson 2014) or Langskaill (Moore and Wilson forthcoming) have challenged the concept of a landscape bare but for the broch 'villages', and allow for a more balanced view of the MIA settlement pattern, yet there is also a clear change in settlement type, which must reflect serious and large scale changes in Atlantic Iron Age society at this time. The brochs give way to wheelhouses (see Armitt 2006) and to the 'Pictish' 'jelly baby' (Ritchie 1977) or multicellular/figure of eight (Moore and Wilson 2014) structures. These are all small scale structures, or at least smaller than the 'Atlantic Roundhouse' type typified by the massive brochs (Armitt 1990, 2005a) and appear to reflect the rise of individual domestic units. Barrett and Foster interpret this change in terms of a penetration of local power systems by more distant and more powerful structures associated with the rise of the 'Pictish' proto state: the change from a ranked society to a larger emergent state (Barrett & Foster 1991; 49).

The appearance of counters at this time is part of a much wider change in the character of material culture. There is a distinct paucity of material culture associated with the early and middle iron ages; one of the 'markers' for the beginning of the LIA(1) is the rise in the sheer number of artefacts and the appearance of new types of artefact, such as items of personal adornment (Foster 1990). Sharples (2003) has commented on this and sought to explain it by linking it to the changes in the settlement forms. For Sharples, the opportunities for personal display shift from building types to artefacts – the pins, combs and other items signal a shift from family units whose power is predicated on land and architecture to a more individual, portable, expression of influence.

In the case of the counters, they are certainly part of a shift in attitudes to objects, and they represent new ways of using material culture, ways where the relationships between objects is as important as the relationship between object and human. Counters are part of a cognitive shift – the utilisation of objects as things to think with, things which drive forward cognition. This is taking place within a milieu where longer distance contacts with remote power centres in Pictland become stronger and more important, and is probably the ultimate source for the importation of these games from Roman Scotland, far to the south.

Finally, my review of prehistoric assemblages from settlements has highlighted one element of artefact research which is seldom explored. It is common for grave goods to be analysed as a group, yet this is not so for settlement sites. The accepted procedure is for separate finds categories, such as flint, pottery, worked bone, coarse stone tools etc. to be split up and sent to separate specialists for analysis. The various reports are then included in the final publication report but it is rare for connections to be made between categories. Some attempts have been made to remedy this (see Sharples 1998, and the National Museum of Scotland's integrated approach to specialist reports, F. Hunter *pers. Comm.*); however the point still stands. The reason this is relevant to the present discussion is that play very often brings together objects of different materials and shapes, and it is only by looking across finds categories that one might spot the evidence for play, or at least the 'playful treatments' of artefacts. I argue, ultimately, (see Chapter 8, final discussion, below) that there is in reality little difference between play and the ways that objects are made use of or encountered in our daily lives. The 'compositions' of objects recognised in the Neolithic midden at Links of Noltland (Moore and Wilson 2011a) are one example of this, as are the astragali from Bayanne (Moore and Wilson 2014), but other examples are no doubt lurking unseen within site archives.

In the next chapter I go on to discuss a form of dice found in Iron Age Atlantic Scotland, and as part of this I have been led on to consider the difference between play, ritual and divination. Before I leave counters, however, I would like to mention that there are similarities between the use of counters in play and the use of objects in some forms of divination. Both can form sets – groups of objects brought together to form a whole, yet retaining some of their individuality. In divination this is most obvious where the objects are diverse and interesting. They might have been accumulated over a long period of time and serve to remind of meaningful incidents – the tooth of a dangerous animal, say, or a stone taken from a significant location (see Junod 1927). The diviner brings the things together as a set and establishes relationships between them much as the game player does, while at the same time acknowledging the meanings and history associated with the individual pieces.

Chapter 5

Dice

Introduction

This chapter discusses another form of evidence for play in the first millennium AD in Atlantic Scotland. My approach in the previous chapter was to examine play objects in terms of the sets which they sometimes form, which usefully focussed attention on the properties of counters and on the ways they are combined during play to create new understandings of the world. I did not, however, dwell on either the context or the archaeological background. My aim here is to investigate a form of play which used 'parallelopiped dice' (a type of four sided die) , in terms of the society of the time and also to ask if the adoption of the dice formed an integral part of wider changes which can be identified as taking place between the 4 to 6 centuries AD. I take the view that the appearance of the dice at this time is symptomatic of these changes and that they (the dice) are part of a change in the way people engaged with objects.

Parallelopiped dice are distinctive artefacts with a widespread geographical distribution: they have been recovered from sites in Shetland, Orkney and the Western Isles as well as northern mainland Scotland (see figures 3, 4). Their distribution can be said to adhere to 'Atlantic Scotland' and is thus contiguous with the associated settlement forms, (particularly 'brochs' and 'wheelhouses', I will describe these in more detail below).

The dice are interesting on a number of levels:

- As objects in themselves.
- Their material properties and their decoration.
- The manner in which they were deposited.
- The archaeological contexts from which they were recovered: the buildings and deposits in which they occur.
- Their place within society.

There has, however, been little interest in parallelopiped dice for more than 40 years. At one time they were cited as part of an argument around the presence/ absence of English migrants in Atlantic Scotland (see Lane 1987 for a good summary of the argument, and a convincing rebuttal) but if they are mentioned at all now, it is not in their own terms but in the context of what they can say about a site as a whole: their presence on site is sometimes taken as a useful chronological indicator, in the absence of secure radiocarbon dating.

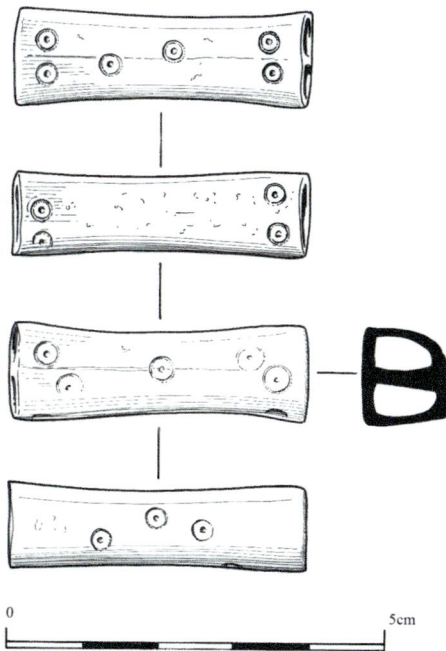

Figure 3. Drawing of Parallelopiped dies from Knowe of Skea, Westray, Orkney (Alan Braby).

Following Dice

One of the themes which emerged from my encounter with Euchre concerned the nature of the relationship between the game and the Westray community in which it is embedded. In that case I found the principle of *following* to be particularly interesting and insightful – just as players follow the cards on the table, farmers follow their animals or crops. I found that there was a way in which people tended to set up the conditions for future action and then follow them as they played out over time. An example would be the way in which a farmer sows the seed for barley and then must follow the outcome over the months ahead. He or she will attempt to affect the result, i.e. the success or otherwise of the harvest, by the implementation of

Figure 4. Parallelopiped die from Knowe of Skea, Westray, Orkney.

PLAYING WITH THINGS

various strategies: manuring or fertilizer use, the use of pesticides and above all the skill in judging the correct time to commence a harvest. This 'following' is layered and complex and is one of the ways this isolated community is connected to the outside world – for example I found one farmer who also 'kept an eye on' global oil prices as well as currency exchange rates (with the euro) because these had a direct effect on fertilizer prices. Farming in a location as far north as Westray, particularly arable farming, operates at the edges of what is possible; the risks which are part and parcel of life here are met with by a combination of bold decision making and subtler management: one takes account of the risks and then throws the dice. The outcome is accepted and the best made of it as one moves forward.

The subject of this chapter is not cards but an unusual form of dice, and they may appear to be very different, however there are key similarities. Fundamentally, both utilise random generators and play must take account of their results, whether it be the hand dealt in euchre or the throw of the dice. This chapter, then, is about chance and its place in society.

Play and Ritual

Any study of play must also be aware of ritual since it is not always easy to define the difference between the two (Raveri 2002; 2-3 and papers in Hendry and Raveri 2002, Bornet & Burger 2012). It is probably more obviously relevant in games of chance, because chance is also a fundamental part of divination: a type of game, if you like, but one which makes use of a 'divine' random generator to explain events, both past and future. A game of chance is also a type of game where there is not always a need for any other player — one plays against luck, and in this sense it can be open ended, one can never satisfyingly win when the opponent is missing; the objects which provide the chance, whether they are dice or cards, seem to play themselves.

In this chapter, then, I am also interested in the way in which the manipulation of chance offers a mechanism by which change can be understood and placed within a coherent framework or belief system.

I shall place my discussion of the dice in the context of ritual and in their wider archaeological context. There are various ways to achieve this but my solution is to begin with a discussion of the relationship between play and ritual and then move on to the dice. I then include a section in which I summarise some of the archaeological trends apparent in my study area, before finally returning to the dice.

Ritual and play

Many anthropologists have commented on the relationship between play and ritual (e.g. Schechner 2002, Turner 1969, Lévi-Strauss 1966, Bornet & Burger 2012). If ritual is essentially a kind of performance — a performative expression of religion —

wherein beliefs are expressed in a concrete form then there are obvious similarities with theatrical performance. Games like chess and euchre are also performances, and have their own theatrical aspects; does this mean that these games are also rituals, or possess ritual aspects?

Lévi-Strauss claimed that there was a key difference, that play had the effect of creating divisions within society while ritual was the opposite: a divided group could be brought together through the performance of ritual. He also stated, however:

> 'Ritual, which is also 'played', is on the other hand, *like a favoured instance of a game*, remembered from among the possible ones because it is the only one which results in a particular type of equilibrium, between the two sides.' (1966, 30, my emphasis).

It is clear that for Lévi-Strauss at least the difference between ritual and play was sometimes very hard to discern, but he seems to contradict himself here because he gives no more information on what he means by 'particular type of equilibrium' and he has already made it clear that for him play always ends in a winner and a loser. It is thus (in his understanding) 'zero-sum', to borrow a term from game theory, and permits no middle ground.

Another possible way to tell play apart from ritual is to ignore the content — on the basis that they are so similar — and look instead at the outcome. Play might be thought of as having an uncertain outcome, while ritual's is predetermined (Bronkhorst 2012). As McClymond points out, however, (McClymond 2012: 155-156, Bronkhurst 2012: 166) this again is not a fool-proof method of distinguishing one from the other.

Victor Turner took another view. He sought to combine his understanding of ritual (Turner 1969) with play in the form of drama. He was interested in its performative aspect, and the use of play in the 'liminal' space created by the ritual. The creativity he associated with play helped to forge new ways of understanding events or tensions which might otherwise destabilise the group. Turner followed play theorists like Huizinga and Caillois in interpreting play as an activity which was set apart, a creative, experimental, zone where the world can be recreated safely. For Turner, ritual and play are above all symbolic and he regarded symbols themselves as events rather than things, dynamic entities, whose performance acted to resolve internal tensions present in society (Turner 1983: 124-125).

Richard Schechner has emphasised the similarities between performance and ritual. For him, the difference lies not so much in purpose as in context, and emphasis (Schechner 2002 [1994]: 613). The relationship is not an opposition but

> 'an interplay between efficacy and entertainment...Whether a specific performance is 'ritual' or 'theatre' depends mostly on context and function. A performance is called theatre or ritual because of where it is performed, by whom, and under what

circumstances...No performance, however, is pure efficacy or pure entertainment. The matter is complex because one can look at specific performances from several vantage points, and to *change perspectives is also to change one's characterization of the event.*' (2002 [1994]: 622-623 my emphasis).

He also concludes 'Ritual is part of the warp and woof of every kind of performance, sacred and secular, aesthetic and social' (p643). Schechner, then, allows for a more nuanced, multifaceted, view of play, one which allows for one play form to contain several interpretations without their having to compete or interfere.

There are many examples of games where play and ritual seem to collide or intermingle. Schechner gives a few and it is not difficult to find others. Trobriand cricket is one well known example of a game taking place in a ritualistic fashion (Weiner 1988), Lévi-Strauss mentions football among the Gahuku-Gama of New Guinea (Lévi-Strauss 1966: 30-32), there is the Mesoamerican ball game (Whittington 2001), gladiatorial contests in the classical world (Plass 1995, Toner 1995), kite flying in Thailand (Mauss 2007), funeral games in the Greek, Etruscan and Roman worlds (Grant 2000, 13-19) or the funeral games of the Fox Indians (Mauss 2007). There are also the funeral games held by Achilles in honour of Patroclus, at Troy. The papers in Bornet and Burger (2012) offer other examples. In these cases, the boundaries have been blurred. A game is co-opted into ritual (Trobriand cricket) or it seems that a ritual arises in the form of play (Mesoamerican ball game) or adopts the play form. The question to ask, then, is not whether these activities are games or rituals but what is their context and how can that context allow a better understanding of the activity, whether it be play or ritual?

It is Schechner's view, and to some extent Turner's, which I find most useful and which I take to the parallelopiped dice. In particular, Schechner's observation that it is context, and point of view, which is important allows for a more nuanced interpretation. At the same time, there are, of course, problems with this approach. Despite its insights into the problems of ritual theory, as Catherine Bell has noted, it continues to regard activity as dramatizing or enacting prior conceptual entities in order to reaffirm or re-experience them. Far from overcoming the dichotomy between doing and thinking, the performance approach, according to Bell, 'appears to suggest a further exaggeration of the structured relations between thinking theorist and acting object' (Bell 1992: 38-39). For my part, I continue to regard play and ritual as somewhat interchangeable, as context-dependent and, above all, as dynamic and reflexive.

Parallelopiped Dice

Most of the dice which are in use today are six sided and cubical, with a standardised form of numbering (opposite faces always add up to seven, numbers represented by dots). A die need not be limited to six sides, however; there are many modern games, such as role playing games, which utilise more unusual types of dice. Dungeons and Dragons, for example, uses dice with various numbers of sides: 4, 6, 8, 10, 12 and 20 sided dice can all be used in this game. Each dice gives a certain probability which, in a role playing game, is suited to a particular task. The games which Woodburn describes among the Nomadic Hadza (Woodburn 1970) utilise two sided dice, as do a few of the games formerly played among the North American native peoples (Culin 1975 [1907]).

Parallelopiped dice have four faces. They are made from short lengths of animal bone, mostly around 40mm in length. They are squarish in cross-section and are about half as wide as long. Most have open sides (a natural consequence of the use of animal long bones above a certain size), thus only the four long sides are available for numbering.

Clarke's account of the dice is the most recent thorough study (Clarke 1970). He rounded up the available knowledge and summarised what was known at that time; he counted a total of 21 dice from around Scotland. Unfortunately, a large proportion of these came from antiquarian excavations or were isolated finds so that it was not possible to discuss their context in any detail. It was possible, however, to show that they have a very distinctive distribution and are confined almost entirely to the Northern and Western Isles and to the north Highlands. Since then, a further ten have been recovered, all from modern excavations. In addition, I include six die excavated from Dun Cuier, which were excluded by Clarke, and one possible unfinished die from Clickhimin broch, which was not in Clarke's corpus but is illustrated in the Clickhimin site report (Hamilton 1968). There are thus now a total of 38 known dice, which form the basis for my discussion.

Clarke was less interested in the form and function of these objects than he was with their place in discussions regarding the origin of certain distinctive elements of Atlantic Scottish Iron Age culture, particularly brochs. The Scottish dice bear some resemblance to English examples, most famously a group from the Glastonbury Lake Village (Childe 1935; 238-42, Mackie 1970, though see also Lane 1987) and had been cited as one element in the evidence for a supposed influx of English migrants during the late 1 millennium BC or early 1 millennium AD, an influx which was thought to have brought with it new types of architecture (brochs) as well as new types of material culture (Piggott 1966). The argument has fallen by the wayside as radiocarbon dating and new excavations have brought new information. Scottish dice are later than their English counterparts, those from the Glastonbury lake village, for example, probably dating to no later than the 1 century AD, at the very latest. Parallelopiped dice are also known from the Roman world, where they most likely originated (MacGregor 1985), but were replaced by cubical dice by the 2 century AD (St. Clair 2003, 114). With the collapse of the argument for English migrants by the early 1970's (Clarke 1970, Lane 1987, although see Mackie 2002; 43-44 for an attempt to cling to the argument, if in a modified form), parallelopiped dice have fallen somewhat into obscurity and are usually only discussed as part of the relevant specialist analysis within a wider site report.

Dating, Context, Condition

Dating

Four recent excavations have recovered dice from secure, radiocarbon dated contexts:

- At Bornais, in South Uist, two dice were found. One (cat. 1973) came from a 'charcoal layer' (457) in 'House 1' (interpreted as a wheelhouse) radiocarbon dated to c500-600AD (see Sharples 2012; 48-49 for dating). This charcoal layer contained charred timbers and is interpreted as evidence for a massive fire which destroyed the wheelhouse (Sharples 2012; 50), it contained a large number of artefacts including the die which was, peculiarly, unburnt and said to have been placed upright within it, after the event (*pers. Comm.* Niall Sharples). The second die from Bornais (cat. 2503) came from a midden layer to one side of the site and can be regarded as contemporary with cat. 1973 (Sharples 2012; 122).
- At the Knowe of Skea in Westray, one die was recovered from the interior of a small building, Structure E, which overlay two burials, one human the other of a cow, which have been radiocarbon dated to the 5 C AD (Moore &Wilson 2011b). The building is not thought to postdate these burials by a significant period of time, given the presence of articulated human bone within its wall core (further radiocarbon dates are awaited). Structure E is a distinctive small building very similar to one from Buckquoy, also in Orkney (Ritchie 1976). Anna Ritchie has discussed the possible religious connotations of this type of building (Ritchie 2003).
- At Scalloway in Shetland five dice were recovered, all from within the broch interior (Sharples 1998; 174). The earliest dice (cat. No's 3999, 6003, 6004) came from a thick layer of ash which spread across the interior and marked the end of the primary phase of occupation. This layer has been radiocarbon dated to the 4 – 5 centuries. All three dice were heavily burned, presumably as part of the conflagration; they may have been lying on the floor when the fire began. One die (cat. 6002) was found in rubble (14) associated with late broch re-occupation and is interpreted as being residual (Sharples 1998; 48). This die was also heavily burnt; its dimensions closely match one of those from the ash layer (6004) and it is possible that they were originally part of one set. The fifth die from Scalloway (cat. 3563) was found in a pit close to a hearth associated with the final broch occupation. This die can be no later than the 7 century, based on a radiocarbon date obtained from a deposit of articulated cattle legs, which provide a *terminus ante quem* for this phase. This dice was not burnt, unlike the others from Scalloway, and was of slightly different proportions, being shorter and fatter.
- Excavations at Pool on Sanday, Orkney recovered two dice. One (cat. PL2992) was not complete and was severely worn. This came from a context associated

with Structure 17, a stratigraphically early building dated to the 3 century AD (Hunter 2007; 82). This building had been badly truncated by Viking phase activity, however, and the SW part had been entirely removed. What was left was damaged by post medieval ploughing. Given this, and the worn and incomplete state of the die, it is far more likely that it is intrusive and should be considered to be contemporary with the other die from the site. The second die from Pool (cat. PL3136) came from occupation deposits within Structure 19, which are dated to as late as the mid sixth century AD (Smith 2007; 514). This dice was complete though worn through use.

Given the above information regarding dating, it is possible to suggest a date for the use of most parallelopiped dice sometime in the 5 and 6 centuries AD. The presence of the fifth die from Scalloway (cat. 3563), which is from a later context, supports the suggestion that there may be a later group of dice, of a slightly different shape.

Context

The association of dice from two sites with distinct episodes of conflagration is curious: the dice from Scalloway and Bornais both came from thick ashy or charcoal rich layers interpreted by the excavator as relating to destruction. One of the dice from Pool (cat. PL3136) was found inside a building (Structure 19) which was also associated with a thick ash layer F274 ('a particularly thick spread of burning': Hunter 2007; 96). Here, the excavator does not make the association with a destruction layer but it is fair to ask the question: was this structure also destroyed by fire?

This link between bone dice and ashy deposits or burning is found elsewhere though the contexts of the dice from other, older, excavations were not recorded in as great detail. Some information is, however, available from the published accounts:

- Six dice were found during Young's excavations at Dun Cuier, Barra. Five of these (Young 1956 Fig 13, 5-9) were found in 'peat ash deposits' near to the hearth, only one was burnt, however (No 5). The remaining die was recovered from 'greasy earth' of the enclosure.
- One of the two dice from the broch of Gurness was found near or associated with a secondary hearth (Hedges 1987).
- Finally, the die from the Knowe of Skea was found next to the hearth, in a type of building which may have cult associations (Ritchie 2003).

Of the remaining dice, not enough information is known about their context/provenance, so nothing can be said about these, yet of those where the context was recorded there is a distinct association between parallelopiped dice and burning or destruction. Of the 18 where context is recorded in sufficient detail, 13 have this association.

Condition

Most of the parallelopiped dice survive in good condition. These are small, sturdy objects and they generally remain complete. Many have polished surfaces, and their numbers can appear worn, as if from repeated handling. Even where they were burnt they remain mostly whole but there is a small number which are heavily fragmented. In a case such as PL2992 from Pool, the die is obviously battered and worn but this die had been disturbed repeatedly prior to its final deposition, and its condition reflects this treatment. In other cases, though — die No. 5 from Dun Cuier; dice 6003 and 3999 from Scalloway; one from Burrian broch; both from Dun Mor Vaul; and Clickhimin — a die is represented by very small fragments. Animal bone is resilient and strong - it bends before it breaks, and parallelopiped dice are strong, chunky, objects. It is difficult to conceive of these dice being accidentally shattered into such small pieces and I would suggest it is more likely that they have been deliberately broken.

Numbers

The numbers on parallelopiped dice were created through the use of 'ring and dot' motifs, where a central dot was set within a larger concentric circle, probably through the use of a small scribing tool, or compass (MacGregor 1985; 60, Sharples 2012). The numbers were placed on each face in an orderly, symmetrical, fashion so that 6, for example, was formed by two groups of three ring and dots at either end of the face; 5 has four ring and dots towards the corners and one in the centre; 4 was formed by two pairs, one at either end; 3 is usually a triangular group in the middle.

The numbering is definitely unusual: they were almost always numbered 3,4,5,6 and usually in that order. Given that there were only four faces available, it seems strange that none are known where the numbering is 1,2,3,4 as one might expect, and it does not seem likely that numbers 1 and 2 were on the ends but have now been lost, for example where a plug of organic material has decayed. There are one or two examples of dice where the ends have been marked but this was probably to distinguish dice in one set from one another (see Clarke 1970, Sharples 1998). The use of numbers 3 to 6 could be taken to imply an awareness of 6 sided dice - these were certainly in use in Scotland at this time, though further south in mainland Scotland.

It is as though these dice were made in awareness of six-sided ones, and that the highest four numbers have been kept and the lowest two discarded. It is not difficult to make a cube from animal bone, the only restriction being the size of the raw material available. In Atlantic Scotland, as well as cattle and sheep being available there were also deer, pig and marine mammals, all of which have provided sources of bone as a material, over many thousands of years (see MacGregor 1985, Hurcombe 2014).

It is admittedly peculiar that these dice are parallelopiped and not cubical and that they are numbered from 3 to 6 rather than 1 to 4. How to explain this? One suggestion is that by numbering the long faces from 3 to 6 the two faces at the ends, impossible to attain during play, are accounted for.

How the Dice Were Used

It is likely that many dice were not in fact used singly but in sets and where more than one dice has been recovered it is noticeable that some can be grouped together by size. Scalloway and Dun Cuier, for example, all exhibit this trend; the dice from these sites can be subdivided into groups of three or four. One of the solid dice from Scalloway (cat. 6002, see Sharples 1998, Fig 111) was numbered 4 on both ends, probably in order to distinguish it from others in a set.

It is less easy to see any real difference between 4 sided dice (i.e. parallelopiped dice) and six sided dice if only one of each is considered. In terms of probability each number on a die (assuming the die is not loaded) has an equal chance of occurring: 1 in 4 for a parallelopiped die versus 1 in 6 for a six sided die. The question becomes more interesting if one considers an activity which uses more than one die. Two 4 sided dice have 16 possible outcomes when thrown together (4x4). Two 6 sided dice, however, have 36 possible outcomes (6x6). The effect of using more dice in a throw is to multiply the number of possible outcomes, rather than simply to add them.

When more dice are added to a throw the range of possible outcomes (how many 4's, 7's or 9's, for example, one gets when one adds the scores from each die) is not evenly distributed, as it is for one die. So, if a single 6 sided die is thrown there is an equal chance that any one of the numbers from 1 to 6 comes up. If two six sided dice are thrown, then a larger number of 7's will occur. Out of a possible 36 combinations 6 will add up to 7 (5 will add up to 6 or 8, 4 will add up to 5 or 9 and so on) and this effect is magnified when more dice are added to a throw.

For parallelopiped dice, if two dice are thrown there is a total of 16 possible outcomes, 4 of which will add up to 9. Thus the effect of combining a four sided die with numbering which runs from 3 to 6 is to limit the number of possible variations and to move the modal value from 7 to 9. If two parallelopiped dice are thrown then it is more likely that they will add up to 9.

As more dice are added to a throw the effect is magnified; parallelopiped dice possess a narrower range of outcomes but have a higher modal value. The person who uses groups of parallelopiped dice will reach more high numbers than if he or she uses groups of six sided dice and, conversely, less low numbers. Also, it is worth considering that where more than one 6 sided dice is used in a modern game two dice are most common and this was probably so in the past. Parallelopiped dice, however, seem to have been used in sets of three and four. These dice would, then, have given quite radically different outcomes from the more common 6 sided dice in use elsewhere at the time, for example in the Roman world.

All of the above assumes identical dice, as are used today and as we expect the dice we use to behave. If the dice are identical it does not matter which one yields a six or which one yields a 4, all that is of interest is the total of the throw. If, however, the dice are considered to be unique identifiable objects which are not interchangeable — that is, where one can maintain a record of which die produces a certain number — then the situation becomes more complicated again. I have also assumed up to now that the dice are not loaded and are completely unbiased, but this is not necessarily always the case, as I discuss below.

Rolling, throwing, placing

These objects are carefully made and some show evidence of heavy use, whereby the numbers have become worn and polished through handling. They are solid, reassuring objects to hold and too large to shake in a hollow made in the palm of the hand, as one can with modern dice. The exact ways in which they were used has been the subject of speculation.

There are several possible ways in which the dice could have been used. Clarke (1970) suggested that they might have been rolled, perhaps on to a blanket or skin, or one person might have hid them while another guessed which numbers were uppermost. They may also have been used as dominoes, or 'rolled' in a dice tower though no such objects have ever been found in Atlantic Scotland. The recovery of a die from Scalloway, Shetland, which appears to have had an iron pin inserted on one face led to the suggestion (Watson in Sharples 1998) that they were designed to be rolled: this die was rolled several times and the conclusion was that it had effectively been loaded by the iron pin (Sharples 1998). This now appears to be the accepted interpretation of their use (see Hunter 2007, Armit 2006, Hall 2007) but even if it does seem likely that they were intended to be thrown it is debateable whether the tiny piece of iron in the Scalloway die really would have had any effect; I would question the validity of the 'experiment' — a random sequence will naturally yield a preponderance of certain numbers, given a limited data set (try flipping a coin 10 times) and no statistical control was undertaken. It is also uncertain whether the use of these objects as dice would even have yielded a truly random number sequence. Animal bone does not have a uniform thickness and although their exterior faces have been trimmed to shape, none of the hollow dice show any signs of internal trimming, which would be essential if one would wish to balance a die. One of the dice from Bornais (cat. 1973, Sharples 2012, Fig. 171) is distinctly curved (a curved piece of animal bone was used) and would have been biased. It is likely that most parallelopiped dice had peculiarities and anyone who had much experience of one would know where it was most likely to land. It remains possible, in fact that the numbers were placed to take account of this bias: the highest value may have been placed on the side which was most difficult to achieve (in the process turning it into more of a game of skill than one purely of chance). I have not been able to test this theory, for although I have handled many of these dice I have shied away from rolling them for fear of causing damage.

As far as use-wear is concerned there are one or two points which may be made, and I would like to distinguish two kinds of wear, or damage.

- Firstly, there are the signs of wear which might be expected to have accrued through use as dice and some show signs of long, heavy use. On a few, the numbers have been worn nearly smooth by constant use and they are polished from constant handling. Some are quite fresh and appear to have been in use for only a very short period of time, if at all, before being lost or discarded. There are no signs of the kinds of slight nicks or indents which one might expect to see if more than one dice were thrown together, or if they were thrown onto stony or rough surfaces. The use wear which I have detected is more consistent with careful but quite intense use. These objects seem to have been used with restraint and to have spent a great deal of time in peoples' hands.
- The second type of 'use wear' which I distinguish may not be use wear at all, in the conventional use of the term, since it relates to the condition of the dice as found. There is a small group of dice which are burnt, and another group which have been broken prior to deposition and I would suggest that it is as likely that in both groups the damage was deliberate and was inflicted as part of their deposition, in order to place them beyond use. The Bornais die, likewise, though not itself burnt, was deliberately inserted into a layer of ash, removing it from circulation.

Atlantic Scotland during the Late Iron Age

In this part of the chapter I provide some detail on the archaeological background to this period. When I looked at euchre on Westray I was able to follow the game out of the hall where it was played into the community it was set in, and I will do something similar here, from an archaeological perspective.

Archaeological approaches to this period have been dominated by broch studies for most of the previous century (see Armit 1990 and Ritchie & Ritchie 1991; 89-121 for background). These towers, together with their associated extramural settlements, have held a powerful place in archaeological imaginations and most accounts of society in Atlantic Scotland between, approximately 500BC and 500AD treat brochs as key: the interpretation of their uses, the artefacts found there, and their place in a settlement or social hierarchy provides a model upon which much else rests. I would argue, however, that much of the debate has been predicated on interpretations which favour certain qualities of some of these monuments; in particular, a view of brochs as strong, isolated and above all defensive has leached into Iron Age studies in general. These interpretations are based on extreme examples, and has skewed our appreciation of society at this time.

Brochs are not the only settlement form during this period and I include wheelhouses and souterrains. I describe each of these settlement forms in turn below.

Brochs

Brochs are massive drystone circular structures which can reach impressive heights. Mousa broch in Shetland, for example, still stands to 11m: its 'cooling tower' profile is often cited as the typical broch shape. Ruinous brochs often form enormous mounds which are readily detected during even the most rapid or casual field survey; they are thus well represented by field records. They can be found in distinctive, spectacular places, for example on promontories, cliffs, hilltops or small islands, and are often enclosed by massive banks and ditches. They were often interpreted purely as defensive structures, however more recent work has led to a realisation that these buildings were primarily used as dwelling places (see Armit 1997, 36).

Most brochs possess one or more of several distinctive architectural features: intramural cells and passages, 'guard' cells in the entrance passage, hollow wall construction, more than one level. They have thus formed an attractive data set: one which contains a range of well-defined attributes by which it may be ordered. Broch studies have, then, historically, tended towards classification and subdivision and consequently there are brochs, sub brochs, semi brochs, duns, semi duns, galleried duns, solid walled brochs, and brochs with ground floor galleries. Many of these classifications can be made without recourse to excavation since the defining features are often obvious – intramural cells and galleries and scarcement ledges, for example, can often be picked out amongst the rubble. Wall thicknesses and internal diameters can be readily obtained. It has, however, also been clear for some time that many classifications are confusing and can be based on quite subjective appreciations of what a broch is, or is not. The difference between a broch and a dun, for example, is not always clear. The term 'dun' sometimes refers to a somewhat ad-hoc fortification of a rocky piece of ground, sometimes it is applied to a small 'broch' type building. This confusion is most obvious in the Western Isles where a very wide range of different architectural forms occur during the same period.

The traditional interpretation, where brochs are acknowledged as a distinct form within a range of similar settlement types leads to confusion because it is not possible to give an absolute definition of what a broch is (see Fojut 1982b for an early appreciation of this problem). This has led to a somewhat confused picture of society at this time: if brochs are the residences of elites, what of duns, for example, or forts or promontory forts and blockhouses?

A more recent approach replaces 'broch', together with its unwanted baggage of classification, with 'Atlantic Roundhouse' (see Armit 2005a, 2006). Ian Armit has traced the development of brochs as part of a roundhouse tradition which is widespread throughout mainland Scotland from the early Iron Age and which develops somewhat differently in the Highlands and Islands, resulting in specific forms such as the brochs (and wheelhouses).

His approach is opposed by those like Niall Sharples (1998, *pers comm*) or Ewen Mackie (2002) who might be said to be in the 'broch' camp and insist that 'broch' is a useful term, one that can be applied to a specific, readily identifiable, type of building. Sharples, in particular, insists that brochs are readily identifiable – that these are a distinct category in a settlement hierarchy. Many other archaeologists agree.

The site of Howe, in Orkney is a good case in point. Here, excavation uncovered a sequence of one 'roundhouse' followed by two 'brochs', built successively one on top of another. It was difficult to define these structures absolutely, except that 'broch 1' survived in good enough condition to preserve a few of the features usually associated with brochs (Ballin Smith 1994; 37). The reasons for interpreting the earliest structure as a *roundhouse,* are never explicitly given in the final report. The final structure is occupied at about the right time for it to have been a broch and during construction its builders handily included some broch type features: intramural passages plus stairs to higher levels. It illustrates the thinking whereby the broch element, as the most important, highest status structure, is implicitly taken to have replaced the earlier ones but not to have grown from it. The history of development at the site is acknowledged but not explored on its own terms.

When Noel Fojut asked 'Is Mousa a Broch?' (Fojut 1982b) he was being provocative but he also usefully analysed the statistics and made the point that according to these Mousa is not a broch because it is in fact not a good example: it lies at the far end of all the graphs. Yes, it possesses guard cells and intramural passages and stairways, and 'voids', but its wall thickness is greater and its internal area is smaller than just about any known broch-type building. This is not to say that Mousa, and the very small number of structures with similar properties, are not brochs, as such, only that the type tends to be defined by the most extreme examples and if one looks back to the lumpen mass of brochs one soon finds many unusual forms. It becomes quite difficult, in fact, to pick out what is typical (see also Hedges 1987).

Atlantic Roundhouse is the more inclusive and ultimately the most useful term, not only because it makes most sense of a large number of important structures, all with their own peculiar attributes or variations on a theme, but also because its use has the beneficial potential to break down apparent differences between Atlantic Scotland and developments further south, where massive 'defensible' settlement forms are also employed, if sometimes on a different scale. The developed roundhouses, or 'homesteads' of Perthshire (see Hingley et al 1997) are a good example. It is also useful because it helps to explain the occurrence of 'broch' forms far to the south outside the usually accepted boundaries: Leckie broch in Stirlingshire, for example, or Edin's Hall in the Scottish borders. If brochs are accepted as roundhouses it allows for a more nuanced appreciation of the development of each site within its particular context. It does not deny that each site is a part of a wider society but allows us to view the form in its own terms.

Beyond this argument, or just lack of definition, there is a broad agreement that Atlantic Roundhouses, or brochs, stood at the pinnacle of *local* hierarchies. Studies such as Foster's (1989) have illustrated, through access analysis, how Atlantic Roundhouses dominated surrounding settlements. Gurness in Orkney is a good example of this with its extramural settlement clustered around the central broch tower and John Hedges' work on Orcadian brochs, particularly Gurness and Bu has been influential. At Gurness, he demonstrated that the extramural settlement here was contemporary with the broch and not a later addition. The early radiocarbon dates from the Bu broch are one of the key developments in broch studies and have helped to demonstrate a long, slow, evolution for this site type.

Wheelhouses

A wheelhouse is a round structure where the interior contains prominent radial partitions – the partitions are likened to the spokes of a wheel and have thus given rise to the name. The cells defined by the partitions may be individually corbelled, leaving a central open space which would have been roofed using timber and turf. The entrance passage can be long and incorporate a guard cell on one side. A peculiar and distinctive property of some is that they are semi-subterranean, being constructed in large holes dug into sand, such as at Cnip, Lewis (Armit 2006), and some were constructed inside the ruins of earlier brochs, as at Jarlshof (Hamilton 1956). Many, however, were freestanding above-ground structures, for example Clettraval, North Uist, and Scatness, Shetland (Scott 1948, Dockrill et al 2010).

There seems to be an obvious contrast between brochs and wheelhouses. Brochs are seen as externally monumental and impressive; they dominate the surrounding landscape. Wheelhouses, by contrast, can be monumental constructions but this might have been appreciated only from the inside, with little to show above ground and with no bank and ditch defences or cluster of extramural settlement. Even where a wheelhouse is not set directly into the ground surface it can occupy the ruins of earlier buildings. There is a sense, in these cases, that the wheelhouse occupied space in a different way to the broch; it is almost absent, its inhabitants occupied a subterranean space which may have been impressive from inside but was effectively hidden from outside view. This has led to an understanding of the wheelhouse as part of the landscape while a broch was set apart from it. Armit has summarised this contrast in terms of structure/environment and in terms of the place of the wheelhouse in its environment and territory (Armit 2006; 252).

Finds from brochs and wheelhouses are, however, remarkably similar: simple stone tools, plain pottery, a scatter of iron work and the occasional more exotic find.

In terms of chronology, wheelhouses are generally contemporary with brochs but many also post-date them. Bornais, for example was occupied until at least the 7 century AD (Sharples 2012). Many wheelhouses are not directly associated with brochs, particularly in the Western Isles but the two settlement forms have often been found together. At Scatness, Shetland, a range of wheelhouse type buildings clustered around the central broch tower (Dockrill et al 2010). In the Western Isles wheelhouses are more often isolated and obviously subterranean. Cnip wheelhouse, for example was built within a massive pit excavated into sand (Armit 2006).

The wheelhouse can also be represented by no more than a series of ruinous piers projecting from the interior wall face of a broch (e.g. Scalloway, Sharples 1998). Sometimes the difference between a wheelhouse and any other roundhouse form is not so easy to discern. The Cill Donnain 'wheelhouse', for example, is poorly defined and represented by no more than a hint of floor and radial partition (Parker Pearson & Zvelebil 2014

I would like to make the same point for wheelhouses as I have done for brochs, which is that this is another architectural form which is defined by the most extreme examples. If most brochs are not Mousa, then most wheelhouses are not like the one at Cnip, or those at Jarlshof. Most 'wheelhouses' are simply part of a development of roundhouse forms visible all over the Northern Isles, at least, since the Bronze Age (see Moore & Wilson 2011a, 2014). All of these forms are united by radial partitioning; some are subterranean, others are not. There is no convincing reason why they should not be classed as wheelhouses except that the term carries too much baggage. What they share is a response to local conditions and a desire to manage space in a certain way.

Furthermore, if one abandons the straitjacket of the traditional definition, it becomes possible to account for strange gaps in the distribution pattern. Orkney, for example, has long been recognised as an oddity because no wheelhouses have been recognised there. The problem does not exist if one accepts the very large number of other buildings which have 'wheelhouse' properties, for example the radially partitioned structures at Knowe of Skea, Links of Noltland and Langskaill, all on Westray. The question then turns not so much to 'is it a wheelhouse?', or 'why are there no wheelhouses here?' to 'what were the conditions which gave rise to these forms?'

Souterrains

Souterrains are poorly understood, however they are included here because they fill out a picture of settlement in the middle Iron Age. Souterrains are underground passages, of varying length and complexity. They can be simple small chambers or long tunnels. Sometimes several tunnels join. Their function is debated: storage, refuge, ritual. They are important because they do not occur in isolation but are part of larger above-ground structures and can be taken as a proxy for a class of settlement which is in itself rarely excavated and little understood.

It is not always appreciated that more lies in the area or that the souterrain is itself one small part of a larger above-ground structure. For all the many souterrains known, very few have formed the subject of comprehensive excavation. Howe, in Orkney, is a well-known exception — the souterrain here was accessed through an entrance in the floor of the early roundhouse, (Ballin Smith 1994). Souterrains are rarely associated with brochs, (although other underground structures are known, for example the 'well' at Gurness broch, or the Mine Howe subterranean chamber). Excavations at Langskaill farm, also in Orkney (Moore & Wilson *forthcoming*) encountered a souterrain together with a small part of the associated house. Enough was excavated here to be able to provide a radiocarbon date of around the 1 century BC for the house and souterrain. Three were excavated at Jarlshof, in Shetland, each of which was found to be associated with a small roundhouse type building (Hamilton 1956).

These structures have been found throughout most of Scotland. A search of the RCAHMS database reveals records of some 834 souterrains (and 772 brochs). Souterrains are often found during farming activities — a farmer might pull up a capstone during ploughing, revealing a hidden chamber. The discovery of an underground chamber or tunnel is distinctive, and memorable, and explains why the locations of so many are known. They are a useful proxy for non-broch settlement and can be used to fill out a settlement pattern which might otherwise be dominated by large, monumental structures.

Broch, Wheelhouse, Souterrain

The combination of broch, wheelhouse and souterrain does not give a complete picture of settlement in Atlantic Scotland: there are a few other forms, such as those at Knowe of Skea, (Moore and Wilson 2011b) about which very little is known. These three elements do, however, serve as a framework, a skeleton upon which more can be layered and their analysis can also give us a good idea of the nature of society and how it changed.

This society is usually characterised as small-scale and composed of small independent units, each with its own hierarchy (or lack thereof). There is no indication of any overarching authority which might have intervened above the 'broch level'. Each separate unit was probably in competition with those nearby. The defensive nature of brochs, with their high walls, guard cells, banks and ditches is taken to imply a degree of insecurity, however it is less clear whether these defences were ever put to use because there is very little direct evidence for strife.

What is clear is that each settlement developed along its own trajectory; the size, longevity and relative success depending on a range of factors, not all of which can be traced to geological or geographical happenstance (contra Fojut 1982a).

The resources available to a locality or perhaps its place on a trade route would have played their part in defining how a settlement developed over time; so would other less easily measured factors, such as relations with other individuals and groups, the role of personality in maintaining trade contacts or simply the skills available to the inhabitants in their everyday encounters with their environment. There is no reason why all of the inhabitants of a particular place should be ideally adapted, so as to maximise the 'return' from their environment, or technology. In some cases the archaeological record reveals that the inhabitants made what appear to be quite poor choices. The collapse of the roundhouse at Howe, due to poor foundations, and the poor condition of broch 1, for example, show how the builders got it wrong, but persevered (Ballin Smith 1994). Likewise, the outer wall face at Midhowe on Rousay was shored up on at least one occasion as the wall began to slump or collapse. One of the wheelhouses at Cnip remained unfinished (Armit 2006).

Changing Architecture

There are many changes in the settlement record, but from around the middle of the first millennium the older, more monumental and longer lasting structures have been repeatedly altered so that by the 5 or 6 centuries it is fair to ask if a broch built in the second century BC should still be regarded in those terms if its defences have been dismantled and filled in, the layout and use of space in the interior has been radically changed and it no longer survives to the same height. In any case, by this point new structural types have begun to appear.

These are small and generally cellular, and more organic, typically with one small space opening off another. Where the interiors of brochs, wheelhouses and roundhouses (attached to souterrains) shared a use of *radially* divided space, the new forms were more linear and the interior space is more obviously *weighted* (Sharples 2003) and less evenly divided. Sometimes these buildings are constructed within the shell of an old broch, as at Loch na Berie (Armit 2006, Harding and Armit 1990, Harding and Topping 1986), or nearby, as at Scalloway (Sharples 1998). Some have no broch associations and were constructed entirely away from the old settlements, as at Red Craig (Morris 1989), the Brough of Birsay (Hunter 1986), Bayanne (Moore and Wilson 2014), Buckquoy (Ritchie 1976) and Pool (Hunter 2007). A few recognisable forms have emerged: the 'Jelly Baby' (a real archaeological term, e.g. Buckquoy, Ritchie 1976 or Burland, Moore and Wilson 2014) and the 'figure of eight' (Red Craig, Morris 1989, Bayanne, Moore and Wilson 2014).

Changing Economies

As the settlement record changes so do other aspects of life in Atlantic Scotland. Julie Bond (Bond 2003) describes the arrival and gradual rise in the percentage of Oats cultivated at Pool, from early in the first millennium AD. By the 6 century, Oats are found in over 60% of the samples from Pool (Bond 2003; 107); this is against a constant, unchanging, backdrop of barley cultivation. She has also detected a change in the faunal assemblage, arguing for intensifying dairy cultivation. She links both changes to improved risk-management; crops are being managed better and new foods, in the form of dairy products, being produced which store better over winter. The adoption of oats may be linked to the intensification in dairying: oats grow well on poorer land and allow for new areas of land to be brought into cultivation; the greater harvests allow for more animals to be kept. Bond also suggests that this entails the first beginnings of an 'infield-outfield system' with barley in the well manured infield and oat production in the rougher outfield. This is a radical departure from the way the land has been managed for hundreds of years and suggests a growing intensification in farming, linked perhaps to a greater pressure on the land.

Changing Artefacts

Further changes become apparent in finds assemblages. The finds associated with early and middle Iron Age sites are remarkable for their 'utilitarian' nature. A typical assemblage might comprise simple cobble tools; pumice, some of which may be worked; iron working debris; a few iron tools such as knife blades; pottery is usually plentiful. The most interesting and varied part of the assemblage usually comes under the heading of 'worked bone' which includes a variety of objects, but again these are usually simple and work-a-day things such as weaving combs, undecorated pins, points, and so on. Most of the finds can be directly associated with agriculture, food preparation, or textile and skin manufacture. Technology is simple with no evidence for the manufacture of very many complex items. The exception is ironworking: this is a new technology which has been widely adopted, yet the objects which are made are small and, again, generally simple.

By the middle of the 1 millennium, finds assemblages have changed. Pottery and stone tools are still found in large numbers, as before, but the difference lies in the growth in new types of objects, such as decorated pins and brooches, arm and finger rings etc. which can be characterised as items of personal adornment. In addition, there is the appearance of composite bone combs, which are complex items requiring skill and possibly an element of craft specialisation to produce. Imported objects appear from further south and the wider 'Roman' world.

Some Reasons for Change

The underlying reasons for these changes are debated. By the mid-1 millennium the brochs have become 'ancestral piles'; they have been passed on from generation to generation for many hundreds of years and it is the manner of this inheritance which, it is argued, led inevitably to their downfall (Armit 2005b, 2006). Armit has based his interpretation on the 7 century Irish model of inheritance and, according to him, the best fit for the archaeological record is 'redistributive partible inheritance' (Armit 2006; 253), his term for a system where the broch and the associated land holdings are held communally within a kin group. Empty landholdings are then passed intact to a descendant in the same kin group. This social structure is essentially egalitarian and generates little change in land ownership and settlement pattern over time. For Armit this explains the apparent stability of the settlement record seen in Atlantic Scotland for most of the first millennium BC and into the first centuries of the next. He does not explain categorically why this system breaks down, however, but only posits a general rise in inequality over time, leading towards the sudden sweeping changes detailed above.

Sharples has highlighted the change in material culture. For him, the rise in items of personal adornment reflects a shift in political power away from these small scale systems towards larger groups located further away (the Pictish 'proto-state'). For him, brochs and their dwellers were at the top of a local hierarchy. The monumentality of the broch, together with its massive defences are taken to point towards a dominant role in local politics where one of the broch dwellers' key abilities was the control of agricultural surplus within a territory, via storage and redistribution. By the middle of the 1 millennium, however, the influence of these larger groups means it is no longer acceptable to express power or influence by the construction of monumental brochs, or wheelhouses. Smaller buildings are built instead and people use objects such as pins, rings and brooches to display their position within society.

Armit and Sharples have each attempted to explain the changes in the archaeological record in particular ways, based on what are fundamentally different interpretations of the nature of society at the time. For Armit, as what was a generally egalitarian society becomes more hierarchical pre-existing patterns of landownership slowly break down under the pressure of internal tensions. For Sharples, the pressure is external and political, and brought about by the rise of the Pictish 'proto-state' to the south.

Both explanations have their strong points. Sharples' might be better at explaining the influx of exotic items from further afield but is based on a rather old-fashioned view of the place of brochs in local hierarchies (see, for example, Mackie 2002; 2, Ritchie & Ritchie 1991 for similar interpretations). Armit's view of the nature of a tension between roundhouse, broch and wheelhouse is perhaps the more nuanced and holistic but does not explain the changes in the composition of finds assemblages in the same way; also, he appears to have fastened upon his inheritance model without very much justification.

It is not certain, however, that these changes all take place simultaneously. If Armit is right, then he has identified a process which might take place consecutively over many hundreds of years in various places all over Atlantic Scotland as each kin group gradually becomes more and more unstable. Each broch, or wheelhouse, would have been built in response to the local circumstances of each kin group but this process would be isolated from others nearby.

It is more useful, I believe, to view the period as a whole as one of gradual change, of movement over time, within which trends are visible as communities maintain contact, sometimes over long distances. The archaeologist's obsession with the monumentality of some brochs has coloured our picture of this past and has conditioned us to expect overarching, large scale transitions leading from one isolated settlement form and economic model to another.

The evidence shows that roundhouse forms develop slowly, however, only occasionally reaching the extremes of broch or wheelhouse form, before evolving into the more organic shapes seen later in the 1 millennium AD. Material culture likewise develops. Not enough attention has been given to the 'ecology' of these settlement forms. All had an intimate relationship with their environment which will have affected their final form. In physical terms this might mean the availability of stone to build up with, or deep sand to dig down into, or a ruinous broch structure to make use of. There are other kinds of environment – the social, for example, - which will also influence the form of the structure as it develops. There was probably in fact no final form as we expect, only something which emerged continually over time. To put it another way, they grew rather than were made (Ingold 2013, 20-22), their final form taking shape within a kind of 'morphogenetic field', the 'total system of relations set up by virtue of the presence of the developing organism in its environment' (Ingold 2000, 344).

It is in this milieu — one of constant slow change, of gradual transition — that parallelopiped dice first appear. I argue that these objects have a significance beyond being only another new type of find amongst many. They do not fit neatly into prevailing categories as, for example, an item of personal adornment. Since they relate to play they may derive from the everyday, be part of the 'quotidian rhythms of personal lives', but this is not certain. My feeling is that their presence exposes yet another change taking place, in the mid-1 millennium AD, which has to do with the relationship between people and things.

Discussion

Parallelopiped dice in their wider context

Most syntheses of this period treat brochs as unproblematic. There is a tendency to see these structures as the remains of a society engaged in constant, if low level, warfare characterised by internecine raiding, possibly for livestock and resources such as cattle and even possibly for slaving. Each settlement was implicitly expansionist, seeking to extend influence and power at the expense of their neighbours. Their location on high, defensible locations together with the presence of enclosing banks and ditches seems to support this interpretation. Common architectural features of brochs, such as 'guard cells' at the entrance, have also led to this viewpoint, and it seems undeniable that defence must be a consideration. This has, however, led to a particular view of these monuments, and, by implication, of the people who constructed and used them.

How was this society organised, however? There is very little solid evidence for violence and it is fair to assume that most people were not in fact constantly fighting. It is certain, in fact that the brochs were dwelling places, where people lived their lives peacefully. The recent excavations at the Knowe of Skea — the first excavation of a broch period cemetery — recovered the remains of several hundred contemporary individuals but none of these showed any signs of trauma (Dawn Gooney, *pers comm*, Moore & Wilson 2011b). Hingley has come close to this view; he has noted the lack of direct evidence for conflict and painted a picture of individuals competing before the walls rather as the ancient Greeks did (Hingley 1992).

I feel it is more productive to view this society in terms of a 'theatre state' (Geertz 1980) than as some kind of 'cold war' stand-off between opposing forces. Geertz's analysis of the competing states present in 19 century Bali identifies a society where 'the struggle was more for men- for their deference, their support and their personal loyalty – than it was for land' (1980, 24). Geertz does not play down the warfare there but places it in the context of a society much more concerned with hierarchy, status and display and does so in terms of performance and drama, instead. For Atlantic Scotland, this type of interpretation has the advantage, I think, of emphasising the active nature of people's involvement with monuments like brochs.

The kind of small scale society which existed in Atlantic Scotland did not have the ability to command individuals — there was no centralised, powerful source of order such as the Pictish state, which replaced it, and the influence which was garnered had no purpose other than its own existence; it was used to build bigger, more monumental, structures, to strengthen defences and to gather rare, exotic objects (for example, the Roman amphora from Gurness broch, Orkney). If we look for a 'purpose' for a broch, or even a wheelhouse, perhaps it is better to view it on its own terms, rather as Derrida viewed play: something which is self- referential and ultimately has little purpose outside of its own existence.

The brochs, and wheelhouses, were also the site of ritual activity. The well at Gurness, for example, with its peculiar hidden chamber or the human remains deposited in the foundations of Cnip wheelhouse are reminders that ritual in this society was not set apart but inextricably bound up with the everyday.

Geertz's analysis is useful because it emphasises the ludic qualities of everyday life — a good background for a discussion about dice, play and ritual (and the lack of difference between them)

Parallelopiped dice in their local context

I argue that parallelopiped dice are not as unambiguously *dice* as at first appears: if one only considered their function as random number generators then one would be led towards an interpretation of them as straightforward, as objects probably associated with gambling or with a board game which perhaps utilised dice during play. A different perspective is gained if, however, one considers the context of dice in more detail. The one from Bornais was set upright, unburnt, into a layer of ash; those from Scalloway were also recovered from a layer of ash and there are hints of associations between dice and burning and destruction at other sites: Pool, Knowe of Skea, Dun Cuier. Some dice were probably deliberately broken prior to deposition. In addition, the die from the Knowe of Skea is associated with a type of building which has been identified as unusual or 'cultic' (see Ritchie 2003). When I look at the context, then, I gain an impression of objects which are associated with conflagration, with dramatic events or places which would have been pivotal in the life of the settlement.

It is also curious that all of the dice are made from animal bone. One might expect stone or even wooden examples to survive (allowing for problems of preservation). Animal bone has its own properties of strength and density which may have made this material more suitable yet its source — dead animals, most likely cattle, may also have been important. In the kind of small scale societies present at this time in Iron Age Atlantic Scotland human-animal relationships were extremely important. An animal's specific history, its ancestors, its personality and character would have been known and remembered and the use of an animal's bones, for whatever purpose, would inevitably have been meaningful.

If, then, one takes account of context together with the material from which they were made and the ways in which dice most likely used, then one is led to view these objects through an alternative perspective; one that brings the relationship between play and ritual into sharper focus.

Dice, Play, Ritual

If parallelopiped dice had a role in a more ritualised form of play, what form did this take? It was suggested that the dice from Bornais were used in a form of divination, where the results of a throw were used to predict future events (Hall 2007) but there is also a use for divination as an attempt to offer an explanation for *past* events. In the context of Bornais, then, it makes sense to see the dice from there as linked to the layer of ash derived from a disastrous conflagration which resulted in the destruction of the building; was the die used as part of an attempt to understand or explain this event?

Divination is a way of accounting for the world, a way to place seemingly incomprehensible events within the grasp of a prevailing world view. I would argue that this is one of the uses of parallelopiped dice and that it explains their repeated occurrence in contexts associated with conflagration, and with their general association with change: something has happened, or is happening, and the dice are part of the ways these changes are understood. As with Euchre, (chapter 3, above), divination is also a kind of following, in that it is a way of tracing the flow of events from the past into the future.

Parallelopiped dice are an unusual type of object; they are very different to those normally recovered by archaeologists, at least in Iron Age Atlantic Scotland, because they are designed to behave in an unpredictable fashion. This must be one of their most attractive attributes and it explains why they must be followed in order to discover their results. In some ways they are predictable - the symmetry used in their decoration provides a level of this (Crowe and Washburn 2004), and if one explores the probability and statistics of dice throws then patterns will emerge. Most other artefact types, however, rely on a greater level of predictability: there is little joy in a hammer stone, or a knife, if it only might, or might not, provide the desired outcome.

If the changes which take place during the mid- late Iron Age can be understood as relating to the individual's place in society and their ability to express such qualities as individuality or status, the rise in objects of personal adornment is similarly linked to the demise of the massive, monumental, brochs, and wheelhouses, as part of an expression of the shift of power away from these localities to a more distant centre. The appearance of parallelopiped dice at this time might be related, but was at the same time an expression of something else: the co-opting of the material world into new cognitive activities, new ways of thinking around objects. The use of the dice was a way for the individual to demonstrate strategic thinking around risk taking, as well as showing their understanding of the events that shaped their world.

Finally, David Riches' account of card playing in a modern Inuit hunting camp makes it clear that a game of chance can also be a leveller (Riches 1975), because the gambling here redistributes valuable items between the players. The context of the gambling is also interesting since, as Riches points out, it only takes place while the men are on a hunting trip — other, more staid, card games are played elsewhere. There are repercussions for the distribution of valuable items. Woodburn's account of gambling among the nomadic Hadza (Woodburn 1970) makes a similar point. Perhaps the parallelopiped dice fit with Iron Age Atlantic Scotland because they act to reduce difference: they move objects around between individuals, cutting across hierarchies when these very hierarchies are under stress and being reshaped.

Play is integrated into life in many different, and sometimes surprising, ways: parallelopiped dice were similarly integrated. In the types of small scale society flourishing in middle Iron Age Atlantic Scotland we should expect to see play as part of peoples' lives rather than set apart. The adoption or invention of specialist gaming equipment at this early stage marks an important change in the nature of play at this place and time; the evidence suggests that the dice were being used as part of wider belief systems not as mere *games*, as we would usually understand the term.

This chapter explored one small artefact type and in doing so it opened up questions surrounding the nature of play and its relationship with ritual. In doing so it also touched on the difficulties of recognising play objects in the archaeological record. In the next chapter I will move onwards once more, chronologically, while keeping my study area the same, and examine an artefact record which is becoming ever more complex and which contains many strange and enigmatic objects. Some of these objects are usually accepted without argument as play equipment, or gaming pieces. If there is a lesson to be learnt from the examination of parallelopiped dice, however, it is that things are not always what they seem. In addition there are types of object which occupy an interesting middle ground between play and other activities. This ambiguity is not purely a result of the difficulties inherent in the archaeological investigation of long dead societies but derives from a genuine quality or attribute that these objects possessed.

Chapter 6

Tafl

In the previous chapter I linked the appearance of parallelopiped dice in Atlantic Scotland to the large-scale transformations in society which occurred in the area around the middle of the 1 millennium AD. I was also able to place the use of the dice in the context of smaller-scale transformations of individual, localised events; for example, the destruction of a house, or room. In this chapter I examine aspects of play during the last quarter of the first millennium AD, however the nature of the archaeological record has led me in different directions and I do not attempt to fit my examples within any overarching framework.

By this time there is evidence for a much broader range of material associated with play, which has been recovered from a range of different contexts, from settlement to burial. Given the range of material it is possible to expand the discussion to address a wider range of questions. Furthermore, other strands of evidence can be introduced, such as documentary sources. It is also possible now to discuss the play with reference to the rules.

Here, my discussion concerns the game known as Tafl ('tables'), a generic name for a group of games which were popular in the 'Celtic' world from at least around the 7 Century AD (Schadler, 2007) until the arrival of chess into southern Europe sometime late in the 10 Century (Eales 2007). In Ireland it was known as Fidchell and in Wales as Gwyddbwyll or Tawlbwrdd. Fidchell and Gwyddbwyll are usually loosely translated as 'wooden wisdom', but Schadler makes the point that Gwyddbwyll is also translated as 'throw board', in the sense that pieces are *thrown from the board* as they are taken (Schadler 2007, 370). It is also referred to as Brandubh, or 'black raven' in Irish sources. There seem to have been two main variants: one where equal sides were pitted against each other, and another where the sides were unequal. The version with equal sides probably derives ultimately from the Roman world and the game of Latrunculi (the 'game of soldiers/brigands' Murray 1952). In the other version a defending side protected a king piece against an attacking side which was twice as large as the defenders. The asymmetric version with a king piece has Scandinavian associations – sets are often found in Viking period burials in Norway as well as in Britain (e.g. Westness: Kaland 1993 and Scar: Owen & Dalland 1999) - and was played by the Laplanders at least until sometime in the 18 century (Linnaeus 1811, 55-58). This is not to say that this was not also ultimately derived from a Roman game; contact between Scandinavia and the Roman world further to the south is indicated by the many instances of Roman glass counters in native contexts, particularly grave fills (Sjovold 1962, 211-212; 1974, Arbman 1943). This version is usually referred to as Hnefetafl ('king's tables').

It is not always clear which game is represented when pieces or boards are recovered from archaeological contexts. In some places, such as Ireland, the two games probably co-existed.

Literary Sources

A few early written sources mention Tafl - there are references to these games in early Celtic tales, (Gwyddbwyll forms the focus for 'The Dream of Rhonabwy' which though set down in the 13 Century reflects an earlier tradition, see Jones & Jones 1998 [1949] xxiii-xxiv, 114-126, see also Jackson 1971 [1951], 152: 'The Magic Gaming Board',), where it has often been mistranslated as chess (Jones & Jones 1998 [1949], 68), but even here the distinction can be difficult to make, partly because it was probably not important what the exact variant was for the purposes of the narrative.

There are also hints in these texts that Tafl had mystical or even 'cultic' associations, which is also seen in a few of the Norse tales and poems. The Voluspa ('the Sybil's prophecy'), in particular, mentions gaming pieces at key stages in the narrative, and it is clear that the game plays a pivotal role in mythology (Page 1995, Palsson 1996, 205-206); these references may relate to a very particular, presumably well- known form of the game.

In some of the Celtic tales there is a distinctive reversal, or dreamlike quality, which is ludic. The Dream of Rhonabwy is perhaps the longest and best preserved example — here the tale records the events of a dream, where the movement of pieces on the board actively affect events away from the game. Thus, the outcome of a battle is governed by the games played by Owein against Arthur.

There are also other, less fantastic, literary references to game playing, (as well as mentions in early Irish and Welsh law tracts, see Schadler 2007); in the Orkneyinga Saga it is counted as one of Kali Kolsson's achievements:

> At nine skills I challenge-
> A champion at chess:
> Runes I rarely spoil,
> I read books and write:
> I'm skilled at skiing
> And shooting and sculling
> And more! – I've mastered
> Music and verse.
> (Palsson & Edwards 1978, 108.)

Palsson & Edwards have translated the game here as chess, however given the early date of this passage (Page dates it to the early 12 century: Page 1995, 167), the confusion between chess and tafl in early sources (Jones & Jones 1998 [1949]), plus the late introduction of chess (Eales 2007) it is likely that Tafl is in fact the game mentioned and 'Chess' in this verse is sometimes translated as 'tables'.

Tafl in Atlantic Scotland

In Atlantic Scotland it is most likely that it was the Hnefetafl variant which was played at this time. This is based on the presence of a number of king pieces and the designs of the gaming boards. The boards often indicate where the king piece, its defenders and the attackers should start from (see Ritchie 2008). There would also have been contact between Atlantic Scotland and Scandinavia from a relatively early date, providing a background of cultural contact within which a game like Hnefetafl would have circulated. It is unlikely, though, that the rules were exactly identical everywhere and there is enough variation in factors such as board design to suggest that local variations existed; Shetland in particular seems to have had a very distinctive version. The basic principles, however, would have been the same over a wide area.

The precise rules of the game were lost for many centuries until the Swedish botanist Carl Linnaeus came across a version of it — tablut — being played in Lapland during the 18 century (Linnaeus 1811, 55-58, Murray 1913, Murray 1952, 63). The rules, as described by him, are simple. A king piece is placed in the centre of a board containing 7 by 7 cells and is defended by 8 men. These defenders must protect the king and enable him to reach the edge of the board without being taken by the attackers. The attackers number 16 pieces strong and attempt to win by surrounding the king on all sides. Individual pieces are removed when they have been 'surrounded' on two opposing squares.

This is a game of strategy, as opposed to a game of chance. Murray (1952) placed it in his corpus with 'war games' but also stated that it has something in common with 'chase games' — here, opposing sides must attain an objective which is not necessarily the same for both sides and not necessarily with reference to the other. The aim of chase games is usually to be the first to gain an objective rather than the one who defeats the other side.

Archaeological evidence for the game has been recovered from a variety of contexts, from settlements, ecclesiastical sites and from burials. Some of these contexts can be interpreted as being of high status, or linked to particular groups, but it is clear that the game is present throughout society and must have been played by a great number of people. It is often associated with 'Viking' settlement and graves yet the early date of some examples makes it clear that it was also played in Atlantic Scotland prior to 'Viking' contact, conventionally dated to the late 8 or early 9 centuries (Crawford 1987, Graham-Campbell & Batey 1998, Woolf 2007).

My own experiences of Hnefetafl began in Shetland and Orkney. Over a short period of time I worked on a few sites which produced good evidence for play, in the form of Hnefetafl pieces and boards: Scalloway broch in Shetland, Sandwick (North) Viking settlement in Unst and Scar boat burial in Sanday, Orkney (see figure 5). These three sites stand out for me, for several reasons: the quality of the evidence was very good; all three sites were very well preserved, as were the pieces, and it was possible to recover contextual evidence surrounding their deposition. The gaming pieces from Scar boat burial were made of whalebone and were found together in a pile in one part of the grave. They were originally deposited in a leather or textile bag, which did not survive. The location of this burial, in shell sand, meant that bone objects survived in excellent condition. The pieces from Scalloway broch were probably the most remarkable because one of the pieces — the king piece — was depicted as small hooded figure, immediately identifiable with depictions of early Christian 'papar' or priests seen on decorated slabs elsewhere in Shetland (the Bressay Cross-Slab, the Papil Cross– Slab and the Monks' Stone, also from Papil see Kilpatrick 2011, Illus 1,2,4,6). Another piece from Scalloway can be interpreted as a probable representation of a broch. The board fragments from Sandwick North were interesting more for their context, since they were found in nooks and crannies around a bench which had stood along one wall of the building; they seemed to have been casually dropped in the course of everyday life, and then left where they lay. These two types of context: the everyday and the special, or ritual, deposit, plus religious association, also form themes for this chapter and I have chosen my case studies because they offer good insights into these aspects of Tafl. I do not discuss Sandwick North here because it remains unpublished, but have included another site, Inchmarnock.

Figure 5. Gaming pieces from Scalloway broch, Shetland (Jenny Murray).

Many Tafl pieces and boards have been recovered from late 1 millennium AD contexts around Scotland. For the most part these consist of individual finds, about which it is difficult to say very much — all that is known is that the game was played in a certain time or place, but it is useful to be able to confirm that the game was widespread. The known examples have been fairly recently summarised (see Hall 2007) and there is not much to add to this, although the pieces from Burland, and Scatness are significant additions (Moore & Wilson 2014, Dockrill et al 2010). I would also include the wooden pieces from Loch Glashan crannog (Crone & Campbell 2005) — the shape of these pieces is remarkably similar to the bone pieces from Scar, and to other glass sets known from Scandinavian contexts and thus may be early examples, from a southerly location in Scotland.

My approach here, given the nature of the evidence, has been to concentrate on three good examples where more information is available. Tafl most likely had many different rule variations and was played in various locations and so my examples also offer slightly different perspectives on this board game:

- In the first, Inchmarnock, Tafl is being played in the context of a small monastic community located on a tiny island off the west coast of Scotland, one where learning and writing are important.
- In the second, Scalloway broch, Tafl has been adapted to express some of the power relationships present within late Iron Age Shetland.
- My third example, Scar boat burial, concerns the placement of Tafl, and other objects, in graves.

All three examples consider Tafl in relation to notation and the ways in which gaming pieces are used to act on the behalf of others, and so I begin by introducing notation, as I have experienced it, before moving on to the archaeology.

From Notation to Action by Proxy

A new element which frequently recurs at this time is the presence of gaming boards, which are found in association with gaming pieces. The surviving boards from Atlantic Scotland are made from stone, and are of various sizes and thicknesses (there is one fragment of a bone gaming board from the Brough of Birsay, Orkney, see Curle 1982). They are rough and ready, generally made from fragments of slabs or thin stones, and usually unmodified. The playing surfaces are incised as a series of interlocking lines to form a grid. It is this rough and ready quality which I have found so interesting, because none appear to have been planned or carefully made (although note the finely made and decorated wooden board from Balinderry crannog, Ireland, as well as the wooden boards from the Gokstad ship burial and Toftanes in Faroes), and it is the boards which have suggested the starting point for this chapter, because they have, for me, brought home the importance of notation, and indicated links between notation and learning, proxy communication and literacy.

On the subject of notation, I would first like briefly to return to the premises of the Edinburgh Chess Club. One of the striking things I found about this place was the presence of large numbers of books, all on the subject of chess. When I first went there I had no great expectations as to how the place would be furnished but I was slightly surprised by all of these books, though of course I should not have been. Games of chess can be recorded by means of a simple, standardised notation: each move is recorded in turn and the game can then be reconstructed whenever one wishes. I found that this process of reconstruction is not always straightforward, because the players want more than a simple record of their moves: they also wanted to know why they had made a move and in the process had to recall their state of mind during the game. This form of notation served as a starting point for the players who wanted to learn about their own games. The books helped the players in the Edinburgh Chess Club learn how other players had acted previously when faced with the kinds of situation they themselves found during play, and to improve their game accordingly.

On the face of it this is the opposite of memory as something which is active – the dry extraction of data from dusty old books does not make the heart race. This is not the whole story, however, because I found that learning to play chess is much more interesting; I found that it most often involved more than one player, that it took place on the board and not just in the heads of those involved, and that it also, most interestingly, encompassed unexpected factors such as emotion. The reconstruction of a player's own old games had as much to do with the reconstruction of his (or her) emotional state since the analysis involved a desire to know *why* a certain move had been made, not just when, and the player was not necessarily completely logical. It helped if the player could remember how he felt, for example, about the opponent at key stages in the game.

Memory also seemed to be 'sticky' — the idea of a rather 'stark' memory where no more was recalled than a record of the relevant moves during the game had no counterpart in fact. The memory was filled out by, or 'stuck' to, many other factors, for example the emotional impact of the game or the ways the opponent reacted during play. Single moves were not recalled; they were parts of strings, longer sequences within which the interesting bits were embedded and it was sometimes more helpful to look for the things the memory was stuck to (rather like cartoon glue) rather than the memory itself since one would come with the other.

I discovered, through chess, that notation is inextricably bound up with learning — one learns about a game, about oneself and about one's own or another's past actions. One also learns how to play.

Chess is complex and the format of longish games in quiet surroundings, makes it quite contemplative: the careful reconstruction of past games is fostered by a game like this. Euchre, on the other hand, as it is played on the island of Westray, is communal, fast moving and noisy. If, at the end of a hand of euchre, one of the players wanted to work out why it had ended in the way it had, much as a chess player might, there would be a quick reappraisal of the cards to see how they had been played. It was important to follow the order of the cards, since the card played by one player would affect the next player's choice. But there was no contemplation here, just a fast check of the cards with queries to the other players to confirm who had played what.

Euchre players learn how to play at the table with others looking on and helping with their choice of card. A few beginners practised at home first, and seemed competent to me, yet this did not eliminate the communal encouragement of those around them. On more than one occasion I saw a more experienced player at one table lean over the shoulder of a beginner at the next table, to advise on which card to play, and this is part of the social side to the game. This can also happen in chess, and I did have (unsolicited) advice shouted at me at the Orkney chess club, but it is generally more unusual here.

Euchre players are not so overtly concerned with past games; in fact it seems to be enough to know that they have been there and played. Whenever I met a fellow player away from euchre they never discussed games or how to play, only whether or not they had seen me at the last meeting, whether or not they might see me at the next. They are content to work with a good basic grasp of strategy and they take it from there. Once the cards have been dealt they have in fact few meaningful choices to make — many hands can pass unremarked until one arrives which has the right combination to 'make something of it'. This is not to downplay the skills of those involved: there are, after all, certain players on Westray who win more often; but they do so, I think, because they have worked out a clear strategy which can be applied to most situations. On more than one occasion my own decisions were queried at the end of a hand, and this always seemed to be on the basis that I had not followed a certain *strategy* correctly. Chess is different — there are of course strategies and tactics but these are combined with a deep knowledge of past games which can be brought to bear on any given situation and, most importantly, a commitment to the situation in hand. Here, when my mistakes were examined, it was important to work through them on an individual basis — what really mattered was how I had reacted to the position as it was presented to me on the board, following my own and my opponent's moves.

Euchre and chess both illustrate a social aspect of learning. Players come together to play in a communal fashion; they learn the game with others, and improve through discussion and practice with others. At euchre, novices would have more experienced players hovering behind them, looking over their shoulders at their cards and offering advice, and there was an oddly similar feeling at the Edinburgh chess club when younger players were present — the room was noisier and people would move around more; it felt more 'bustling' than contemplative, for all that the young players were being tutored.

I thought it would be interesting to look and see if I could trace something of my experiences of notation and learning in Chess and Euchre in the archaeology of Tafl. I was, however, immediately struck by the fact that notation in games, in the sense of how it is used in chess, does not seem to exist prior to sometime around the late 18 century. Philidor's book of chess games (1820) is one of the earliest systematic attempts to record past games. I would, however, like to consider the game itself, as it is played, as a form of notation. The movement of the pieces on the board would then be an active representation of the game as it stands at a given point in time, with some evidence of past moves plus indications of future possibilities.

One other interesting point which I took from the Edinburgh Chess Club concerned the ways in which they made use of chess notation, which was not, for them, an abstract list of numbers and letters. When players wished to examine a past game they didn't simply read the notation, but enacted or performed it. They took pieces and a board, set them up and then followed the old game on the board, using the notation as reference. As they worked through it, they frequently pointed out to each other where a variation could be applied, and might explore the possibilities for a few moves before returning to the original notation, or continue on the new track, amending and adding to their notes as they did so. I believe this points to the notation as an active resource for the players rather than a representation.

My experience of chess and euchre suggests that there is a complex, reciprocal, or reflexive, relationship between the pieces on a board, or cards on the table, and a player's mind. The player *follows* the game out there in the world as much as the movements of the pieces shadow some internal, mental, game. There is a risk of falling into the well-trodden path of *psychological* board games studies, where the thought processes of the players are taken to be purely internal and thus merely *expressed* by their interaction with the pieces. This model has given rise to an entire sub-genre of experimental psychology (usefully summarised in Gobet et al 2004). My approach has been from an ecological standpoint and as such I have been interested in the relationship between individual players, between the players and the game, and in the wider setting of the play as it takes place outside of a laboratory.

A board game can be viewed as a form of communication between players, carried out via the medium of the pieces on the board. Given that board games like chess and Tafl involve more than one player it is essential that each player displays his or her intentions to the other and they do this using the pieces to communicate. It is a deliberately confusing system where each player must take account of their opponent's moves and predict their intentions purely by reference to the pieces on the board. This is the heart of any game, where one must use objects, and allow them to 'do the talking'. It is also why the game must be followed on the board and not kept entirely in the mind. This system involves action, but at a distance: the pieces represent the players on the board and the interaction of the pieces stand as a proxy for the interaction of the players.

Action by proxy, where the will or intent of the person is mediated or achieved through an object, is an alternative to assigning agency to objects. What does it mean to act by proxy? It seems that it must be related to agency because it has to do with the situated action of individuals, yet when players engage in a board game they choose to use objects to realise their intent. This, of course, is what human beings do quite generally, when they enrol objects into their engagements with the world around them. Alfred Gell, it will be recalled, had recourse to the notion of secondary agency to characterise the agency of objects, such as works of art, enrolled in the realisation of primary human intentions (Gell 1998). But this notion is inapplicable to chess pieces, which are not considered by players to be agents at all, but rather to stand in as proxy for their own actions. On the other hand, Clark and Chalmers' concept of an 'active externalism' (Clark & Chalmers 2010 [1998]) applies quite well to the relationship between pieces and player. As parts of the environment, the pieces can have 'an active role ... in driving cognitive processes' (Menary 2010; 1). These objects help the player work through the problem at hand. At the same time they function for the player as an extrasomatic means of acting in the world. Following Clark and Chalmers, then, it is perfectly possible to speak of the intentional agency of the individual player, without having to project this agency onto inanimate objects.

This is not the whole story, however, because while gaming pieces are not said to possess agency – and the players I encountered did not treat the pieces as if they did – they still possess properties which allow them to influence other pieces on the board. Chess is the best example of this. Here, one chess piece may directly affect another, for example, place the king in check or threaten to take a rook. There is a kind of mesh or latticework of interconnecting pieces on the board, where the movement of one changes the overall pattern and where the will or intent of the player is manifest within this lattice and brought to bear on the play through the movement of the pieces.

In addition, each piece also indirectly influences and is affected by every other piece on the board, through their *position* on that board, which changes as the pieces around them move during the game. This influence is a result of their being placed on a board; the pieces have been made part of a system where position is relevant.

The archaeology of Tafl

Learning to play at Inchmarnock

The collection of gaming equipment from a site on the small island of Inchmarnock, in the Clyde estuary, is probably the largest yet recovered from Scotland, comprising at least 35 boards but only a single gaming piece (Ritchie 2008). The site comprises an early church together with graveyard and was excavated to a high modern standard. It is relevant that this site was excavated recently, by a professional organisation, because it allows a greater degree of confidence in the findings when compared to some of the older sites: Jarlshof, which yielded a similar, if smaller, assemblage, was 'excavated' in the mid-20 century by workmen with no archaeological training (Hamilton 1956). The gaming assemblage from Inchmarnock is dominated by the boards. These are flat pieces of bluish slate (Dalradian schist) which must have been to hand in the vicinity of the site; many are water worn and were probably picked up from a nearby beach. The designs are simple criss– cross line drawings: shallow scratches which appear to have been executed quickly without too much forethought and without the use of straight edges or rulers. Not all of the boards are for Tafl type games, there are also boards for Merrels or nine-men's morris and alquerque. As a whole, the assemblage spans the 7 to the 13 centuries AD.

One of the fascinating things about the Inchmarnock assemblage is that some of these stones include other designs and there are yet more decorated stones, which do not have boards depicted. There are figurative designs and texts in Latin, ogham and runes. There are also cross incised stones, presumably some of which were once grave markers, and more sculptural pieces, many of which were recovered prior to the archaeological excavations. Many of the slates were used as trial pieces, either to practice writing, in Latin letters and in ogham, prior to their transfer to other media, or, in at least two cases, to attempt Gothic letters before transferal to an illuminated manuscript. Many of the gaming boards also contain fragments of script or designs; sometimes these can be teased apart as layers, one on top of another, sometimes the designs appear to respect one another. One of the best known of the pieces from Inchmarnock is the 'armoured warriors' slab, which appears to show an ecclesiastical figure, complete with house shaped reliquary shrine, being taken in chains to a waiting ship. It may be a contemporary depiction of a Viking raid.

In the published account the discussion of these slates has been divided according to the type of design as well as manner of execution (Lowe 2008). Thus, sculptural stones, gaming boards, non- text/figurative and text-inscribed slates are treated separately by different specialists. For the purposes of this discussion I consider the assemblage as a whole, and place the evidence for play within the context of the site. My reason for this is that I feel it gives a much more rounded appreciation of the role of play here and allows for some more interesting insights into the kinds of activities with which it was associated. The boards and the piece thus sit alongside some 34 pieces of sculpture and more than 100 pieces of incised slate, including those stones which were recovered prior to the modern excavations. The excavator has identified the site as an early monastic settlement (Lowe 2008, 249), founded perhaps sometime in the 7 century around the influential and charismatic figure of saint Ernan. The conventional approach to an assemblage like this is to treat the play as somehow aberrant or unrelated to the rest, however I would argue that they have much in common, based on the manner of execution, as well as on their function. All are forms of notation, and on this basis I would compare the gaming boards to the text-inscribed pieces and even include those that show narrative drawings.

The carvings have been made in the context of a religious settlement; most likely by resident priests or monks but also by scholars, perhaps as young as seven, who were being educated there. This is a literate place with evidence for at least three different forms of writing: ogham, Latin and runes. The individuals who lived there, as at any monastic settlement, agreed to abide by an explicit set of rules, which furnished a system of meaning for their lives. Monastic settlements are orderly and bounded; Inchmarnock was no different, even if it was small and relatively unimportant. The locations or positions of people, buildings, activities and graves and so on was controlled and was set within two concentric valla. Movement around the settlement was regulated by pathways. I would make the comparison between this form of settlement and the gaming boards found there — the system of constraints provided by the boards, and by the rules the monks chose to live by, both function to provide meaning to that system; to cheat or step outside the system is to make it meaningless and invite censure.

It is clear that the incised slates have something haphazard and ephemeral about them. It is extremely lucky that they survived at all; even more is it a testament to the skill of the excavators that they were even recognised as finds: it is not easy to distinguish faint designs on dirty stones during an excavation. Most of these stones appear to have been picked up, used for a short while and then abandoned. Few show any signs of preparation, such as trimming or surface treatment. The method which was used to create the designs relied on a contrast between a weathered blue grey surface and the lighter, fresher, mark exposed by the lines. The exceptions here are the grave markers and crosses, which saw a much more considered execution and were presumably intended to be used, or visible, for a long time. For the rest of the material, there are shades of euchre here: in euchre the cards are snatched up and used, then fed back into the pack in a whirl of movement; this activity is fast and active and concerned more with the process itself than with the result. Likewise, on Inchmarnock, the process of drawing, of writing and of playing, was most important. These activities were focussed: on the creation of an image, the mastery of text, on winning the game, but the media used were haphazard — stones picked from a beach to function, briefly, as gaming boards or paper. For the writing, and the drawing, there is a sense that these are practice pieces, trials and preparations in the creation of skills to be applied elsewhere, and the excavator identified several pieces which show the presence of pupil/teacher relationships. One showed a line of text written, presumably, by the teacher with the pupil's attempt to copy it below (Lowe 2008, 136-141, Cat IS36, Fig 6.21, Fig 6.25, Plate 6.3). There is no clear example of this for the gaming boards, although a few are so poorly drawn that they may have been created by a child.

For the games, there might seem to be no 'end use' of the skills honed at the Tafl board, yet these skills include strategic thinking and valuable social skills. Inchmarnock was not an isolated place, for all that it is a small island and the monastery relatively unimportant. It was connected via the church to a wider world of scholarship and the people who were trained there, perhaps including the children of high status individuals, went on to work and live at other places around the British Isles, at least.

One other point I would like to make about Inchmarnock concerns the pieces which were used to play on the boards, or the lack of them. A single gaming piece was recovered by the excavations, which is surprising if one considers that one board would require at least 25 pieces to play a standard game of hnefetafl. Why were so few recovered? There should have been hundreds. The reason must lie in the nature of the evidence rather in the excavation methodology, which was good. Most gaming pieces were probably no more than pebbles picked up from the surrounding ground surface. Once they had been dispersed from their context they would be impossible to identify unless they remained together. Just as the raw materials for the boards were picked at random, so were the pieces. This again characterises the nature of this activity on Inchmarnock as haphazard and ephemeral. It also reveals something of the relationship between play and objects. The players are surrounded by objects, only some of which might be brought into the play world. Objects are brought in and out of focus as play things according to the disposition of the players. This recalls, I think, Schechner's discussion of performance and ritual (see Chapter 5, above) and his recognition that 'to change perspective is also to change one's characterisation of the event' (2002 [1994], 622-623). At Inchmarnock, the attention of the players had been brought to bear upon simple stones, or perhaps pot sherds, or other ephemera, and their perspective changed. For a short while these objects were treated as play things, things to think with and to act with within the frame of a board; and as much as the monks were *bricoleur* (see Chapter 4 above, Wynn 1994) then this was bricolage, and when the monks' perspective had changed the constituent parts, the gaming pieces, were then eventually simply permitted to fall back out of focus as gaming pieces, to reassume their previous identities as beach stones, or pot sherds.

Playing Tafl with Brochs

Tafl in Shetland appears to have been played in a slightly different fashion than elsewhere in Atlantic Scotland during the last quarter of the 1 millennium AD. Four sites (Scatness, Dockrill et al 2010, Mail and Scalloway, Sharples 1998, and Burland, Moore & Wilson 2014) have yielded good evidence for a version of the game which must have been quite formalised. The pieces used are very interesting and consist of three types: a simple cone, a kind of 'truncated cone' which is slightly larger and has sloping sides and a flat top, and a figurative piece (Illus. 3, 5). The figurative piece was most likely the king piece.

The truncated pieces are very similar in broad shape to broch towers, which although out of use by the time this game was being played, would still have formed very visible and dominant features in the landscape. Mousa broch survives to a height of 13.3m, which is close to its original height, but it was not the only proper tower to have been built in Shetland: Culswick broch on the Westside, for example stood to c 8m high until as recently as the 19 century, before being robbed for building stone, (Mackie 2002), and there must undoubtedly have been more. Of the other brochs, some may have been the focus of reuse during the Pictish period, as at Scatness and Scalloway, and others would not yet have assumed the rounded, eroded mounds they form today. The broch sites, which were once the residence of local elites, probably continued to be important even as their inhabitants' influence declined under Pictish rule, as is indicated by the frequent coincidence of early Christian churches and Viking period activity with these places. The truncated pieces also show some details which may refer to broch construction. The one from Scalloway has criss-cross lines on its upper surface which appear to be roof timbers. That from Burland has an odd incised groove which may be an illustration of an exposed intramural passage, much as is visible on the upper floor of Mousa broch today.

The figurative pieces bear a definite resemblance to the priests depicted on an early Christian cross slab and the side slab from a shrine, from Papil and the Bressay cross slab, from Shetland (see Kilpatrick 2011, Illus 1, 2, 4, 6). These hooded figures have been identified as papar (Lamb 1995), some of the first Christian priests to come to Shetland and who formed settlements in several places, most famously Papil in West Burra but probably also in other places, for example near Cunningsburgh (Old Norse: 'kings place'). Mail, where one of these figurative pieces was found, is near Cunningsburgh.

The resemblances between brochs and truncated cones and between figurative pieces and priests, cannot be accidental. It is likely that Tafl here was deliberately modelled on two of the most influential groups or individuals present in Shetland society at the time. The Tafl was not directly a form of action by proxy, however there is something here, where the pieces have direct representational links to their contemporary society which is reminiscent of it. The meanings of this resemblance are not entirely clear. It may have been an entirely straightforward correspondence but it is as likely to have been taken from a slightly playful or even satirical viewpoint. The brochs, for example, would have been mostly ruinous by this point in time; the roofing timbers outlined on the Scalloway piece were massive and immensely valuable and may have been one of their defining attributes. Were the brochs (and by implication their occupants) being lampooned as the locations of vast, ridiculous expense, now fallen into disrepair? The hooded monks appear solemn but may have been remote, incomprehensible figures engaged in strange, esoteric activities.

These objects are being used as proxies not just for the players but also in a sense for wider groups and individuals. It is a use of material culture for which it is difficult to find any parallels elsewhere in Atlantic Scotland prior to this point. The parallel is often drawn with chess – the adoption of the queen piece in the early medieval period in Europe is said by Marilyn Yalom (2001) to be a reflection of real changes in society at that time, when the queen was more influential. Other chess pieces can also be said to reflect, or be metaphors for, real people or groups – the warders biting their shields in the Lewis chess sets, for example, are often said to depict berserker warriors. Here, in Iron Age Shetland, Tafl is being used in a similar way but at a much earlier date.

Buried Tafl

In my previous two examples I looked at cases where, firstly, Tafl was part of learning within a monastic community, and where the game shines a light on the ways that objects move in and out of our area of focus, or attention. In the second example, Tafl had been adapted to express some of the power relationships present within late Iron Age Shetland. Here I examine the Scar Viking boat burial.

My third example concerns play objects again, and placement, but in the context of graves, which are very formal, constrained types of deposit. Here, the size, shape and location of the grave, the choice of grave goods and the placement of bodies and objects in the grave(s) have been carefully considered. Graves are a good example of 'structured deposition'. Parker Pearson (1999) has discussed the interpretation of burials in archaeology. He emphasises the importance of the living – it is they who create the burial, and who manage the grave into the future. Parker Pearson's experiences excavating Bronze Age and Pictish burials in South Uist has usefully highlighted the fact that burials are not necessarily sealed forever when they are closed but can form the focus for further activity for tens or even hundreds of years following the initial internment. Sometimes the initial burial is deliberately disturbed as part of this process. The grave can be reopened and grave goods and body parts removed or repositioned, as part of what might be understood as the continuing funerary rites (as opposed to grave robbing). This type of activity has been recognised for many years in Neolithic contexts, where communal burials in chambered cairns (Isbister tomb in Orkney, for example, see Davidson & Henshall 1989) were subject to sorting, where body parts might be rearranged or perhaps even removed subsequently for deposition elsewhere. Very often, archaeological examples highlight the layered, sequential nature of burials. In a modern cemetery this is usually ordered on a regular grid system, with some depth of reuse in each plot. In prehistoric examples flat cist cemeteries might be covered by barrow mounds, each containing a single cist, which in turn form the focus for further, 'satellite', burials. Cemeteries, especially barrows, form visible elements of the landscape and guide future activity in the area. Each burial effectively refers to previous ones, slowly constructing a complex web of relationships, which are altered with each new arrival and its interaction with the previous occupants. There is a very real sense in which burial mounds continue to accumulate, to grow and become ancestral as they are returned to repeatedly.

There is a trend in Britain, as a whole, for gaming sets to be found in graves, though this is more common further south. The earliest examples are known from Romano-

British and (Romanised) La Tene contexts (see Stead 1967 for a four player game from a burial at Welwyn Garden City and Schadler's (2007) discussion of the Doctor's grave at Stanway), and the practice continues into the Saxon period (but seems to have died out by Anglo-Saxon times, perhaps as Christian burial practices become more widespread, see Youngs' (1983) discussion in the Sutton Hoo publication). Further north, in Scotland, it is rarer. The Waulkmill hoard most probably derives from one (or possibly more) 4 century, or slightly earlier, grave (Hall forthcoming, Richard Bradley pers. comm.); it is also possible that the pieces from Clatchard Craig (Close-Brooks 1986) accompanied a burial. Hall's corpus of gaming pieces from Scottish contexts includes a smattering of individual pieces, mostly antiquarian finds, which might have derived from graves (Hallow Hill, St. Andrews, for example, Hall 2007, 45). It is not until around the 9 century that gaming sets can be found more frequently in Scotland, in 'Viking' graves. As such, they form part of a custom which can be traced over much of the North Atlantic at that time.

Several Viking period graves are known from Atlantic Scotland, and more are found each year. A few were probably isolated burials, for example the one at Kiloran Bay, Colonsay (Graham-Campbell & Batey 1998, 118-122), the 'Giants Grave' in Fetlar, or the female grave inserted into the ruins of Gurness broch. The presence of a very large cemetery on Westray was deduced from antiquarian accounts and a smattering of finds surviving in museum collections (see Thorsteinsson 1968) but others are known, for example Westness, in Rousay (Kaland 1993). The Westray cemetery was once thought to be one of the most extensive Viking period cemeteries outside Scandinavia, with at least 17 burials, however the very large number of boat shaped settings, some 72, recently identified on the island of Balta, Shetland must now count as the largest (Turner *et al* 2013). The scale and exact date of the cemetery found on Papa Westray, Orkney, during early 2015 is not yet known, however it includes at least one boat burial and a 'warrior' grave (pers. comm. Rod McCullagh). Viking period graves and cemeteries are much better known from Scandinavia, where there is a large corpus of associated material (see Arbman 1943). It is not unusual to recover gaming pieces from these contexts and they conform to a broad type, whatever the material used, bone, glass or metal. They are usually hemispherical with a flat base. Sometimes the pieces have a hole in the base, for the insertion of a peg. King pieces are distinguished by a larger size or by the addition of a small metal fitting. The sets, if complete, can be divided into thirds — one third defender plus two thirds attackers — plus a king piece, and are thus intended for hnefetafl. A few Scandinavian graves have yielded large numbers of gaming pieces (see Arbman 1943) and more than one set may sometimes have been present.

The finds from Viking graves are for good reasons often viewed as a key to understanding the dead person's status, accomplishments and beliefs as well as their sex/gender (Crawford 1989, Ritchie & Ritchie 1991), even if interpretations can be somewhat circular and should be used with care, as Price has pointed out (Price 2014,

179-182, see also Gilchrist 1999, 67-69 for a similarly sceptical perspective on Anglo-Saxon 'warrior' burials); for example it is not usual to question gender association when certain objects are present in a grave.

The presence of weapons is a good indication of a warrior status, and the individual was probably male. If keys, weaving equipment, or brooches, are found the dead person was most likely a woman, who also had certain responsibilities as head of a household. Tools, for example blacksmithing tools, show that the person possessed a trade, skills and status. Exotic items could be the residue of successful raiding — or trading — trips. Gaming pieces can be viewed in the context of one of the dead person's accomplishments and as evidence for leisure activities.

The grave goods, the tools, brooches, weapons and gaming pieces were all made use of as a kind of notation; they represented something. They would have illustrated for those present at the funeral something of the character and achievements of the dead person and if the items chosen to accompany the dead bore a variety of meanings, many were also of a personal nature and were probably strongly associated with the achievements and personality of the dead person. An individual like Kali Kolsson, for example, whose nine achievements are listed in the poem I quoted earlier, might have had those achievements commemorated in his grave in some way.

The Scar Viking boat burial, Orkney, is no different (Olwen & Dalland 1999). This was a difficult excavation, on many levels, being physically located right on the edge of the present day coast, on the island of Sanday. Part of the boat had been washed away leaving the remainder exposed in the low wave-washed edge at the top of the beach. The burial comprised the remains of a man, an older woman, and a child, all placed in a small boat together with a large number of grave goods, some of which were probably old and worn at the time of burial. These objects may have been difficult to dispose of in any other way – too well preserved to just discard, too many associations with the deceased, both personal and religious. At least one object, the sword, was deliberately broken before being placed in the grave. They were used at the funeral as a physical reminder to the survivors of something about the deceased's life and affiliations.

It is striking how carefully all of the various objects, and the bodies, had been deposited in the grave. Attention had been paid to the relationships, and they were placed in strategic locations. Thus the man and his equipment were together at one end and the woman at the other. The boat itself had been carefully prepared beforehand. It was propped upright in the grave cut with stones and part of the interior was blocked off with more stones. The boat was clearly important as a vessel, and no doubt possessed metaphorical power for the afterlife and the journey undertaken by its occupants. The grave itself formed a backdrop and a frame for this process, conferring a particular kind of meaning and I would make a comparison with the gaming board here. These objects are like playing pieces and acted as proxies, on behalf of the dead person and of the mourners.

The middle section of the boat contained the gaming pieces, which lay in a small pile against the side. They were very well defined, and well preserved. Here, 22 pieces were found near the adult male. They were made from cetacean bone and were hemispherical in shape. One was slightly larger and had a small piece of iron inserted into the top. It is most likely that these pieces were used for hnefetafl. No board survived. It is not certain that there was one, but there could easily have been one made from wood, or perhaps leather, which did not survive.

Hnefetafl is mentioned several times in the sagas, and is known to have been regarded as a suitable accomplishment for a nobleman (Page 1995, 167-171). This is an echo of the references also seen elsewhere in the 'Celtic' world, in early Irish law tracts for example, where the game is valued as an exemplar of a certain kind of courtly skill. The nature of the game perhaps appealed to Norse sensibilities: the brave king with his smaller band of loyal defenders bravely fighting to reach their goal (the edge of the board), but it is also satisfying and sufficiently complex to hold the attention.

Hnefetafl is, famously, referred to in the Voluspa, the 10 century poem which deals with events leading up to and following Ragnarok, the end of the Aesir (gods). Here, the Aesir played Tafl during the golden age, before the coming of the giant-women, and then again at the end of the poem, following Ragnarok, when golden gaming pieces will be found once again: '*afterwards wondrous golden gaming pieces which they owned in the early days will be found there in the grass*' (Palsson 1996, 89).

Page noted that the game probably had cult associations (Page 1995, 206-207), and Palsson mentions a theory that the Aesir were believed to possess magical gaming pieces of gold by which they controlled the world (Palsson 1996, 89), which may be one explanation for the repeated association of gaming sets with pagan graves.

My own interest in this lies not so much in this 'cultic' aspect to Hnefetafl, or in the association with graves as such; my point here is that these are clear examples of a very structured type of deposit (see Hill 1995), and that even allowing for the problems associated with the interpretation of graves in general (Ucko 1969), the presence of gaming pieces is illuminating. I would like to step back from the gaming pieces and look at graves like the Scar burial as a whole, and interpret the entire deposit as a kind of game of strategy, one that has been caught as the game is in progress. It is a form of tableau and can be read in terms of notation. I would like to emphasise the way in which there are relationships between the bodies and the objects interred with them as well as between the objects themselves. The grave is composed of sets much as a board game is: there is the set formed by each individual with their grave goods and the grave goods can themselves be grouped into sets: the spindle whorls, shears and weaving baton are grouped together spatially and thematically, as a set of textile equipment. The same is true of the weapons: sword and arrows are together. The gaming pieces were found tightly packed together in a heap and would originally have been held in their set by a leather or textile bag. Combs, brooch, weights also were linked physically to their respective owners. A wooden box, which was almost entirely destroyed by soil processes probably held another set of perishable items, which did not survive. As a whole, then, the grave formed the background, the board, to several sets, some of which may be viewed as opposites or as comparable: the man's weapons vs. the woman's weaving equipment. The child, frustratingly, is absent here because the circumstances of the burial meant that very little survived of the area where he or she was placed. Taken as a whole, the grave should not be thought of as static but as more dynamic, where there is tension between the objects and the bodies. It is a kind of bricolage (Lévi-Strauss 1966), or kaleidoscope (Ingold & Hallam 2007) but also a kind of game, even if it might have finished by the time of the excavation.

Chapter 7

Awkward Objects

This chapter is less about 'play' *per se* than it is about the objects that we play with and how they are identified on archaeological sites. It derives from a major challenge which emerged during this research: how exactly does one recognise play in the archaeological record? How does one tell the difference between play and any other, perhaps more 'utilitarian', activity when one cannot talk to the people who used these things? As part of this research I have considered many objects which initially seemed playful but which I ultimately decided could not be included and which I was forced to discard. I have also, however, asked if some things that were not usually considered as gaming pieces might not be interesting from a ludic point of view. I think this is the opposite to most studies, where one might begin with the gaming piece and only then go on to consider its properties as an object, and in most instances this might be sufficient — I am thinking of the Lewis chess pieces, for example, where discussions begin with their identity as gaming pieces and then move on to consider other aspects – iconography, context, source materials etc.

Instead of looking for the qualities of the object as gaming piece, therefore, in this chapter I examine the possibility that there is a quality of the gaming piece in any object. To put it another way, I have asked if play might be thought of as a universal affordance (Gibson 1979) or even a material property (Ingold 2011) of a type which is not usually considered in discussions of material culture.

Many objects can seem to be play related but on closer examination the boundaries become blurred and more confusing. This is why this study begins chronologically when it does; in the context of Atlantic Scotland during the 1 millennium AD, where there is a wide range of 'material culture', neither gaming boards nor the pieces used are unusual; a few Viking period burials contain sets of objects which can be readily identified as gaming pieces; objects like parallelopiped dice can be classed as gaming pieces, even if they may sometimes be used in less obviously *ludic* ways. These playful things sit within a background of objects which are usually identified as utilitarian: querns, pounders, grinders, iron knives, bone tools, pottery etc. There are also, however, objects and groups of objects which do not readily fall into either camp; there are even a few site types which can be read as ambiguous: in chapter 5 I briefly mentioned a performative side to brochs but there are others, for example Burnt mounds, Shetland promontory forts, or Northern Isles stack sites, which do not fit neatly into prevailing settlement models and have been ignored for more than a quarter of a century (Lamb 1980, John Hunter's excavations at Landberg in Fair Isle were inconclusive, see Hunter 1997).

The process of elimination was at first disheartening – entire periods of prehistory were abandoned one by one in my search for play things and I began to wonder how I would find any good solid evidence. Ultimately, however, I believe this to be one of the most interesting results of all because it points towards a side of play and games which is usually ignored or passed over in the search for the well-defined and more easily understood (though see Sutton-Smith 1997 for an alternative take on ambiguity in play), and I do not think that I would have encountered this quite so strongly if there had not been an archaeological component to my study. This is because archaeology deals with the physical and if one looks at play from this perspective one is forced to consider objects and their uses, and their materiality, first.

Also, it is undeniable that the archaeological process favours certain kinds of evidence over others. As I have stated elsewhere here, I believe that play is a fundamental human activity, and so, if asked why my evidence begins with the early 1 millennium AD I have two possible answers:

My first answer is that the evidence for play in earlier times was of a similar nature to the later material (for example gaming boards, dice, pieces) but has not survived due to the vagaries of soil conditions, archaeological practice and general catastrophe. I do not believe this, however, and so turn to my next answer.

My second answer relates to the fact that there are many forms of play but they do not all leave the kinds of evidence which archaeologists can categorise as play related. The kinds of play which took place during the Bronze Age or Neolithic in Orkney, for example, might not even be recognisable as play to our modern, post-industrial, Western gaze. It is striking that so much of the evidence I have described can be traced to Roman (and ultimately Greek) antecedents and I wonder whether this may be due to a real watershed in play behaviour which can be traced to Roman contact with the Atlantic world late in the 1 millennium BC, and which gradually worked its way northwards. Now, two thousand years later, our perception of what it means to play and of how we play, has been subtly but irrevocably altered and it is difficult for us to recognise a materiality of play which does not entail the use of gaming boards and pieces. This chapter, then, can be seen as an attempt to trace these ways of playing which we no longer recognise as such, and yet still, even in our own world, take part in.

Awkward Objects

I call the objects I discuss in this chapter *awkward* because they refuse to behave – these are things which defy attempts to say *what* they were used for, even if they obviously were *used*, and so will not sit in any of the available categories, at least the ones that archaeologists like to use. They are intransigent or inscrutable: they are difficult to pin down; they straddle more than one category and so also indicate avenues of enquiry where these categories can be challenged. Here, the boundaries between play and non-play, and the place of objects in the articulation of these boundaries, can be investigated.

My initial response to the problem was straightforward. In the first instance, where I encountered objects that I found difficult to categorise, I mentally set them to one side while I got on with those I could more easily identify as play-related and over time I accumulated a long list of oddities — things which seemed to be neither 'fish nor fowl', which did not fit into any of the categories currently used in archaeological reports.

I discuss painted pebbles and Shetland discs in most detail because they are probably two of the most distinctive types of awkward object I encountered and because they cohere as groups of objects in time and space. I could have included others — carved stone balls are another very clear type of awkward object.

My aim here was not really to decide whether a particular type of artefact should be classed as play- related, although that is part of it. Rather, it has led me to question the usefulness of a distinction between play and non- play and brought me full circle to a reconsideration of one of Huizinga's key claims, made some 80 years ago, which I had always discounted as rooted in a rather old-fashioned view of culture, which was that 'culture arises in the form of play' (Huizinga 1950). Unfortunately, he never fully developed what his view of culture was. For him, it seems to have been a given, something in need of no explanation. The examples he used, however, make it clear that he was interested in what might be termed 'high culture', particularly the arts and drama, and that he traced this form of culture to the classical Greek and Roman worlds. For Huizinga, 'Greekness' or 'Romanness' was created and sustained in these playful forms. Huizinga was, however, working at a time when 'culture' had different connotations and for him, the concept seems to have been unproblematic and straightforward.

When I encountered Huizinga's theories I was at once attracted and at the same time put off by this obvious lacuna in his argument; my experience of awkward objects has, however, led me to ask if there is not a sense in which he was right and, in order to do so, I want to sidestep the thorny issue of culture and concentrate on objects and how people use them instead. The presence of these 'awkward objects' has led me to question whether it is always possible to tell the difference between play and non-play and, given this, it has also led me to consider whether those things which are normally considered as purely non-play — a stone pounder or a quern stone — might not also possess qualities more usually reserved for gaming pieces. These include attributes such as:

- Portability and movement,
- Rules surrounding their use or placement,

- Notation,
- The creation of notional interrelationships between objects, or sets, and
- Action by proxy.

Thus, play is implicated in all aspects of daily life, not set apart but more a way by which people approach and use all kinds of objects.

This section is not about modern classification, but something more fundamental. It is about how objects are and were used, how we encounter and make use of things. There are undoubtedly many problems with the ways objects from archaeological sites are analysed and discussed, particularly with the way the categories to which they are assigned tend to divide bodies of material which have much in common. There has been much discussion of this problem and some solutions have been attempted (e.g., Sharples 1998), but I do not pursue that particular problem here because it has more to do with archaeological practice and less with play.

I have divided my awkward objects into three different types:

- The first type includes objects which do not sit easily within archaeological categories. Partly, this is a problem of classification and includes things which can be said to have been 'used' (they might exhibit 'use-wear') but which have no known purpose. Most stand out because they seem to be in the 'wrong place'; they have arrived on a site from elsewhere but cannot be confidently associated with any 'formal' type of use such as a tool might be.
- The second type of awkward object is related to the first but is distinguished by surface treatment or a degree of alteration. There is still, however, no obvious purpose and so play must be considered as an explanation.
- The third type is perhaps the most interesting, because this includes everyday objects which seem also to be used in a ludic manner. This is reminiscent of some counters - for example modified potsherds. The difference, however, lies not in the way that these are objects which have been modified so much as the way they have been used. Also, this does not have to preclude the other more utilitarian uses with which the object is usually associated. Quern stones, for example, are utilitarian objects which nonetheless crop up in a variety of odd contexts. In the recent past, their use was associated with rules which governed their movement (in Orkney it was considered bad luck to rotate them anti-clockwise or 'widdershins'). In prehistoric contexts quern stones are associated with a range of unusual patterns of deposition.

Awkward Type 1: Found Objects

In order to begin this examination of 'awkward objects' I return to site. This is, after all, where most are found and it is also where I spend much of my time, as a field archaeologist. If it is sometimes difficult to know how things were used in the past, the problem begins here. This is the 'coal face', the working end of a long process whereby objects which have not been seen for hundreds or thousands of years are uncovered and eventually integrated, via the archaeological process, into our modern world.

It often seems to be assumed that the things that archaeologists find on site present themselves in an unproblematic manner to the excavator, and much of the literature seems to confirm this — artefacts are discussed as though the detail of their context and purpose, their identity, is a given: a pot is a pot, it was recovered from a certain type of context and its function can be deduced without too much trouble. In most cases this may be sufficient, however if we scratch a little deeper we sometimes find that all is not as it seems.

I start with manuports because they are a good way-in to how archaeologists think and work on site. The term 'manuport' is a neologism which is sometimes applied, essentially, to 'natural' objects which are found on site but which seem out of place: they can be seen to have been brought on to the site – imported - but usually bear no sign of human modification and have no apparent purpose. The word derives from a conflation of two Latin words, 'Portare' meaning 'to carry' and 'Manus' meaning 'hand' — these are things which have, quite simply, been carried by hand; were moved from one location to another. If a purpose could be found then the object would be assigned to a category — vessel, tool, waste, raw material etc. Manuports are usually stones, which are sometimes easily spotted due to their exotic geology. An example might be a beach pebble found on an inland site. Of course, further research into water-worn stones might at some future date reveal a purpose for which this object was kept, but for now it remains a manuport: a thing which may have had a purpose but which until more specialist analysis is carried out can only be characterised as having once been the focus for some unexplained human attention in the past. The term could also be applied to other material types, some types of organic materials (for example cetacean bones and sea shells) often stand out, although these are most often classified as 'raw material'. I first came across the term working on Northern Isles sites in the early 1990's, I think because it was used by C S T Calder, an archaeologist active in the mid-20 century, who had spent much of his digging career there. It is not universally used in archaeology, but it is occasionally useful.

Manuports are a good example of how ambiguous material culture can be. Much time can be spent on site trying to decide what exactly it is that an excavator has just found. A problem can be quickly resolved but if there is a query it is usually because he or she has little experience of a particular artefact type, or of the local geology/ soils formation processes; or it might be that the excavator has not worked on a site of that particular period before and has not encountered the kinds of things which are associated with it. What the manuport does, essentially, is acknowledge that archaeologists work on 'difference': we spend our time on site acclimatising ourselves to local conditions and trying to spot what stands out from the background, what is different. Thus if I am excavating in an area it is not so much that I may be an expert in the material culture of a time or place that enables me to locate finds or detect changes in soil conditions, but that I am continually learning about the current soil conditions and looking out for when they change, either because an artefact has been found or past activity there has differentially affected local soil-formation processes. A pot sherd does not present itself as a vessel fragment but as a change in texture or colour or as a regular shape in the ground. One might think one would know instantly that it is a potsherd, and it sometimes feels like it, but I would argue that this is not the case.

The manuport also acknowledges that things do not always fit the categories we work with on site. Excavation is an orderly process whereby the elements that comprise the site are continually cleaned, assessed, recorded and removed, hopefully in a logical order. The aim is not to understand the site while it is being excavated, although a certain degree of interpretation is essential. It is usually impossible to understand a complex site fully while the work is underway but the post-excavation processes, during which various specialists analyse the data, will result in the best possible interpretations, which will often supplant any understanding the excavator thought he or she had while on site. The aim on site, then, is to excavate in such a manner that the post- excavation can be allowed to progress smoothly, to provide a framework into which the more detailed analysis which follows can be slotted. Artefacts are usually removed quickly, with a certain amount of information, in order to allow excavation to progress at a reasonable speed. It is at this stage, when the artefact has been found, that some of the most important information is appended. On most sites a certain amount of sorting takes place during excavation — the finds begin to be placed into useful categories for future analysis. Thus the finds begin to be grouped thematically: flints are labelled as such and kept together, or worked bone objects, or pottery, or stone tools, or steatite, or charred plant remains, etc. because this is how the specialists themselves deal with the material. There are, of course, many exceptions and even tugs of war between specialists — the flint specialist may also want to examine the coarse stone tools or even the worked bone if they have been worked using knapping technologies (the coarse stone tools specialist or the worked bone specialist never wants to examine the flint). The pot specialist may want to examine stone vessels. A particularly nice find may fall between categories, for example what to make of a ceramic object which is not a vessel? The problem is well known and has given rise to several solutions. The National Museums Scotland sought to study whole assemblages at one stage. Niall Sharples chose to treat the assemblage from Scalloway broch thematically, according to use. There are many seminars and conferences designed purely to get people talking to each other, to bridge the gaps in understanding which can arise around the varied assemblages. Ultimately it falls to the excavator to join the dots between the various specialist reports since he or she is the only person with a sufficient overview and is usually the author of the final report.

The impression I would like to give is of a system which is more fluid and forgiving than it at first appears but which still has its blind spots. Manuports are one of these.

I would like to give one example of a manuport. Most are simple cobbles and not very interesting, so I have chosen a suitably ambiguous one. This is a smallish stone slab which was found during the excavation of an Orcadian site. The site was not particularly complicated — an eroding broch located on a small coastal promontory at one end of a bay. Several trenches were excavated to explore the deposits and to assess the date and condition of the remains. One small trench located to one side yielded several interesting finds, together with structural remains. One of the most intriguing objects to emerge was a stone slab, one face of which was covered with small circular depressions. When this was found, work on site stopped and everyone gathered around while we tried to work out what it was and if it should be kept as a 'find'. The problem with it was that there was no pattern to the circles and they looked very similar to the kinds of marks limpets can make. Close examination (everyone took turns to peer hard at the stone) showed no obvious signs of working. The slab was waterworn and so had obviously been brought from the nearby beach. On the other hand, there seemed to be too many circles to be limpet marks and it was a loose slab whereas limpets favour solid rock surfaces that will not be moved by wave action. The debate as to what this thing was raged on for at least an hour, and was continued later, however a consensus could not be reached. My own opinion at the time was that it was a natural, but interesting, formation which had been brought on to site partly because the slab was of a useful shape and size and partly because of the patterning on one face. It never reached the final report but it has been kept and I saw it in the store recently. I now find that my opinion has changed and that I am more prepared to accept this object as a find, but I still don't know what it is, or what it was used for and I still find it hard to accept that the circles are artificial, yet they must be. Its placement on site was probably important, and it would have accrued relationships with people and with other objects in its vicinity. It may have been used as a proxy. Should it be interpreted in play terms? Is it a gaming piece?

Awkward Type 2: Surface Treatment: Painted Pebbles and Shetland Discs

Painted Pebbles

Painted pebbles are smallish, white quartzite pebbles which bear a variety of designs marked on their surface in a dark brown or black pigment (see figures 6, 7). The first time I encountered these objects was during post-excavation work on an assemblage of finds from a large Shetland broch site. A waterworn stone had been treated as a find, and brought back to Edinburgh with the rest of the assemblage for further work. There was no obvious sign of use wear but it was dirty, and the fact that it was water-worn implied that it had been brought on to the site for a reason (the site lay on top of a hill, where water-worn stones would not naturally occur). It might have

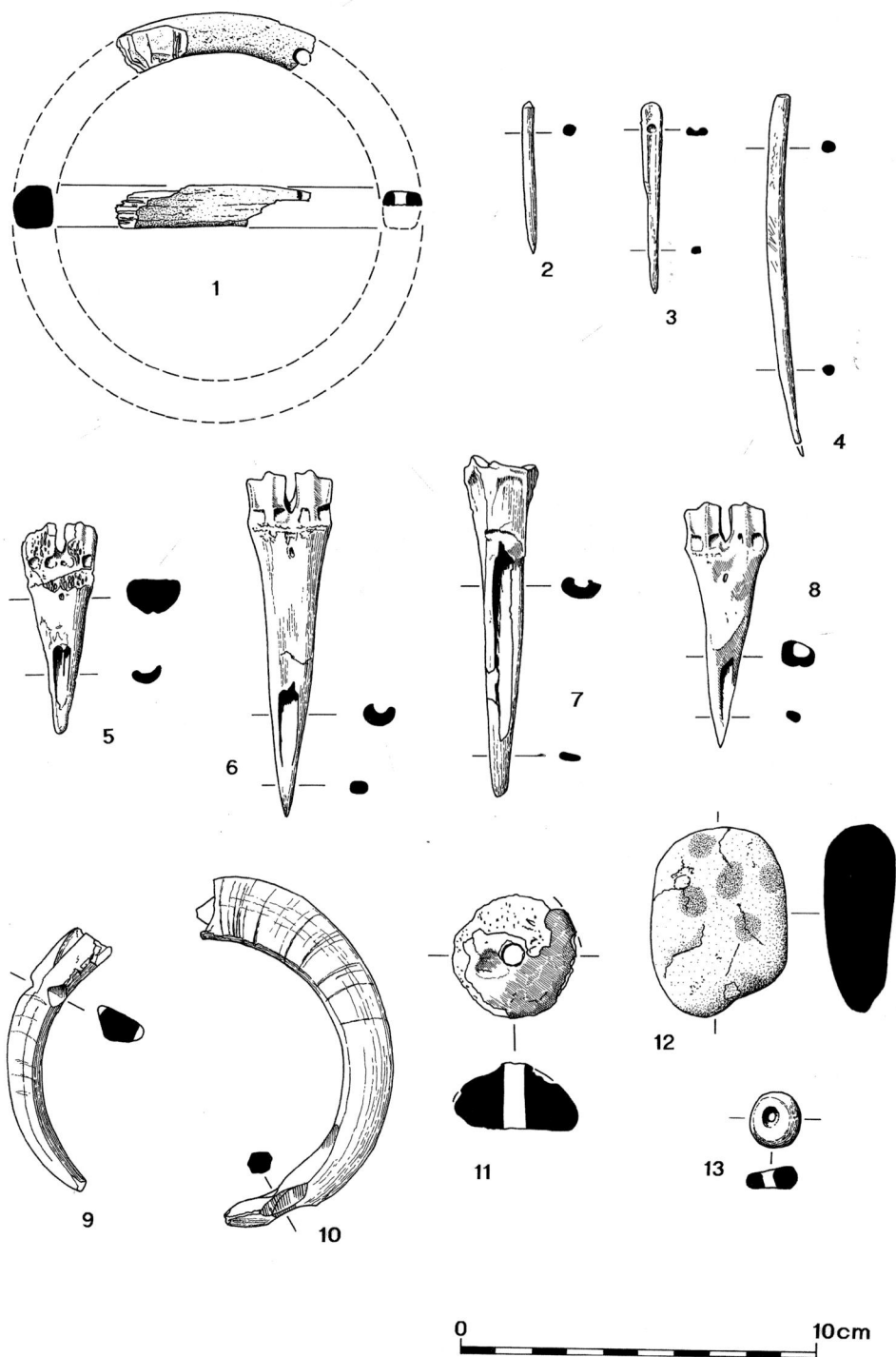

Figure 6. Selection of objects from Bayanne, Yell, Shetland including Painted pebble (Alan Braby).

Figure 7. Painted pebble from Bayanne, Yell, Shetland.

been a manuport, however the most likely explanation was that it was a cobble tool such as a pounder or grinder. These tools are ubiquitous on broch sites and often bear very slight signs of wear which can only be seen properly once cleaned. It was during heavy scrubbing with a nail brush that the stone was found to be a painted pebble, fortunately the pigment is very tough. The source of the pigment is not entirely clear, however recent work has detected lamp black in two painted pebbles (Ambers 2010).

Most of the designs on painted pebbles are simple and consist of no more than a series of dots or lines, or squiggles. They appear to have been drawn quickly, with a brush, and usually no pattern can be discerned but there are a few exceptions, where, for example, a cross has been drawn, or where a line is long enough to begin to appear as if it is not merely random. In a few cases there seems to have been more than one episode of painting on the same pebble (see Burland, Moore & Wilson 2014).

Various explanations have been offered for these objects. One of the most popular is that they were 'charm' stones or possessed some 'amuletic' quality; another is that they were egg decoys for wild birds; there is also an association between quartz pebbles and early Christian burial. There is very little evidence, however, to support any of these explanations and none particularly accounts for their recovery from domestic sites.

Painted pebbles are therefore another awkward object. Should they have been included here as gaming pieces? The stones do not exhibit any signs of use wear and it can be assumed that they were not utilitarian objects in the sense that most tools are considered to be. If they were not tools then what were they? If they were not used to strike or to be struck (as in an anvil) how were they used? The presence of the decoration is intriguing and sets them apart from most of the artefacts which are recovered from sites of this period. The stones might have been chosen only as a convenient background upon which a design could be placed, but then perhaps the decoration was intended to identify the stone in some way. The stones certainly function as a serviceable medium: the designs are still visible today after nearly 1500 years and can even be quite visible when they are retrieved during excavation, the milky whiteness of the quartzite forming a stark background to the dark pigment. However, if it was purely the design which was important one might expect some consistency between stones, a vocabulary, even if the exact meaning is illegible to modern eyes. The designs on the pebbles do not seem to make any sense, however. The use of the pebbles purely as background seems unlikely then. On the other hand, the stones do not seem remarkable other than in that they are all water worn quartzite pebbles generally of a size to fit readily into the palm of one's hand. They must have been imports to certain sites, given the local geology. The third option is that when the pebble was brought together with the design it was the combination of the two that was important and that it was the way this artefact was used which set it apart from other, more utilitarian objects.

In this sense it does not really matter that painted pebbles might not have been gaming pieces in the more accepted sense if we can say that their placement was important and that their movement from one place to another was also important, that they had relationships with people and with other things. If we can identify these properties in an object is this a gaming piece? Or is it an object which behaves much like a playing piece – does this collapse the distinction between play and other types of behaviour?

Shetland Discs

Shetland discs are flat stone discs which measure some 7-10cm in diameter and around 1cm in thickness (see figure 8). Some 16 are known, all of which have been found in Shetland. A lead disc from the Brough of Birsay is similar, though unique, (see Curle 1982, 48-49, Illus 30), plus there is one from Stemster in Caithness but this also probably originated from Shetland (Scott & Ritchie 2009, 3). All are chance finds for which no good provenance is available, although a few have loose associations with broch sites. One was recently recovered from the beach in front of East Shore broch, Dunrossness. It would be impossible to date these objects but for the fact that a few are decorated with simple geometric motifs (Scott & Ritchie 2009) or have Pictish symbols incised on one face. They are therefore most likely contemporary with painted pebbles, and were in use at around the same time as Tafl type games were popular.

Figure 8. Sandstone disc from Jarlshof, Shetland. Diameter 6.87cm (Jenny Murray).

These are large, slightly unwieldy objects, very different from the kinds of things usually accepted as gaming pieces. For archaeologists, at least, gaming pieces are more often small, light things which fit easily in the hand to allow their rapid movement around the board, and can be found in sets, while the discs have only ever been found singly. Like the painted pebbles, they occupy an anomalous position in archaeological discussions and are almost never mentioned except as part of the corpus of Pictish symbols: Shetland discs are of some slight interest here because they are one of a small number of portable objects which occasionally bear these symbols. I have never encountered any attempt to understand these objects (the discs) on their own terms. Usually it is their decoration which is of interest and this is most often discussed in art– historical terms (see, for example, Henderson & Henderson 2004, 88-90).

So, what to make of Shetland discs? Of all the objects discussed this is the only kind which I have never encountered on site, although I have seen them in museum displays and in the collections of the Shetland museum. They are fascinating, odd things which demand some kind of explanation and are my third type of awkward object. Compared to painted pebbles, or manuports, they come closer to a modern concept of what a gaming piece might look like, yet they still refuse to conform. Like the painted pebbles, they occupy an interesting grey area where their function appears to be to carry information, rather than something more overtly utilitarian. The combination of form, decoration and context would have conveyed the information and on that basis they could be classed as gaming pieces, yet I felt that I could not treat them as such. My reasons for this were that they were too big and did not seem to be used in sets.

There are similarities between Shetland discs and painted pebbles, even if is not clear why some were decorated, or what the significance was of that decoration. There are differences also, since not all discs are decorated, although it should be noted that 'undecorated painted pebbles' (admittedly a contradiction in terms) do occur, though they are usually discarded on site as unworked stone (unless they are identified as manuports!). The nature of the decoration on the discs is different, however. On Shetland discs the decoration is regular, considered and obviously references other forms present at the time, not just on Pictish symbol stones but also on metalwork, worked bone and manuscripts. Painted pebbles appear to have been decorated swiftly, without forethought, and on occasion the patterns were added to.

One other object group I will include here, if briefly, is decorated bones and stones. A small number of decorated cattle bones, mostly phalanges and astragali, have been found on archaeological sites in Atlantic Scotland. They have been recovered from sites in Orkney (Pool: Hunter 2007, 509-513, Illus 8.8.25, the Bu Sands, Burray: Lawrence 2005, Broch of Burrian: MacGregor 1974, 88) and from Bornais in South Uist (Sharples 2012, 266-270, Figs 168-170). They all date from the third quarter of the 1 millennium AD. The decoration varies: sometimes it is abstract and geometric, sometimes figurative. One has a Pictish V-rod and crescent and the phalange from the Bu Sands has a 'Pictish Warrior' drawn on it. Excavations at Scalloway in Shetland also recovered an undecorated phalange which had been modified so as to allow it to stand on its proximal end (Sharples 1998). Are these gaming pieces? In his discussion, Sharples linked the decorated astragalus from Bornais to the parallelopiped dice from the same site and interpreted them together in terms of divination: the marks on the astragalus were a record of past throws of the dice. Though an interesting speculation, there is no sound basis for this link, and these objects remain ambiguous. It is also true also that they sit within a corpus of small stones which have been inscribed, sometimes with Pictish symbols (e.g. the arch and V-rod on SF9101, a small pebble from Old Scatness: Dockrill et al 2010, Fig.6.5.4) but more often with incomprehensible graffiti.

Awkward Type 3: The Wrong Context

My third type of awkward object includes those things which seem to be ordinary but which are found in extraordinary circumstances. Assemblages of finds from graves are one example of this, however I discussed the Scar Viking boat burial in the previous chapter so I thought I would use other examples to expand the discussion.

The phenomenon generally comes under structured deposition and it is something I have come across frequently. In terms of my own personal experience the excavations at Links of Noltland, in Orkney, provide several good illustrations of such awkward objects.

The Links of Noltland is an area of eroding dune and machair located on the north coast of Westray. Excavations there since 2006 have uncovered a range of structures and deposits dating from late in the fourth millennium BC until the first millennium BC. The site comprises houses, cultivated soils, middens, burials as well as other more specialised structures. It is a large site, extending over some 4ha and can more generally be characterised as a substantial and well preserved fragment of prehistoric landscape (see Moore & Wilson 2011a).

The preservation is very good at Links of Noltland and a large number of artefacts have been recovered. In particular, the presence of shell sand has permitted the preservation of a wide range of bone material and allowed for a much more complete picture of Neolithic and Bronze Age activities at this site.

It is not unusual to encounter objects which have been deliberately placed in intriguing positions. For the most part these are everyday things which would normally be considered as tools and utilitarian, or waste items. It includes fragments of animal bone set upright in house floors, articulated animal bones and entire animal carcasses in closing deposits. Animal skulls are often found in wall cores; one building contained 28 skulls placed together, as a foundation deposit; polished stone axes are often found in key locations inside buildings, as are complete pots, artwork and figurines. One area which is worth mentioning here is the middens.

The middens at Links of Noltland were at first interpreted in fairly simple terms as areas of waste disposal; however as excavation has progressed it has become clear that there are objects which have been deposited together with others and that associations between the objects and between the objects and midden are important. Furthermore, the discovery of paths and working areas within the middens has shown how these parts of the site are as active and changing as any other. An example is the discovery of a small cattle skull found with a scallop shell placed between its horns. A piece of worked flint was found in the shell. Another example is groups of bone mattocks found together in one area of the midden. These assemblages are found throughout the site and have been termed 'compositions' in the interim report (Moore & Wilson 2011a). They illustrate the collection, curation, arrangement and deposition of objects as part of people's daily lives. Complex series of considered actions often took place over extended time periods; these entailed planning, forethought, and design.

It is usual for archaeologists to interpret these kinds of activities in terms of ritual, however, given the uneasy relationship between play and ritual, should they not equally be thought of as examples of play? Or at least as playful or ludic interactions with objects? When I encountered examples of these types of deposit I was struck by the similarity between them and play. There is a recurring sense of ordinary objects being placed in locations where they gain a sense of meaning from their surroundings and where they obviously have relationships with other nearby objects, as do the pieces on a board; these objects have been co-opted as proxies for human intention, in much the same way that gaming pieces are during play.

Finally: some very awkward objects

There are awkward objects and there are *very* awkward objects. I found these ones very awkward partly because they occur singly or in very small numbers, and not in sets or assemblages, which makes them more difficult to analyse. For the most part, however, the problem here is that they appear to deliberately mimic other objects and so this group includes miniature things, smaller versions of the real thing, as well as life-sized examples.

Examples of this kind of object include the Bronze Age sword shaped object from St Andrews and Deerness parish, Orkney (Ovrevik 1990 [1985], 143 Plate 7.7) which is life size and of a recognized metal type but made of yew wood. There are also miniature things, such as the bone 'knife' from Bronze Age contexts at the Links of Noltland, Orkney, and other small bone 'swords': the swords from Cnip in Lewis and Howmae, North Ronaldsay are both Iron Age (Hunter 2006, Trail 1890). A fragment of a stone ('siltstone') sword was recovered from Old Scatness (Dockrill et al. 2010, 248-249). There is also a terracotta bale (of wool?) from Dun an Iardhard, Skye, which is usually interpreted as a Roman period import (Hunter 2006), and a miniature steatite 'battle axe' from a Bronze Age house at Sumburgh, Shetland (Sharman 2000, 86). Other, more recent, examples I encountered would be the late Viking or Norse miniature quern stones found in contexts in the Northern Isles, as well as the Faroes and Norway.

There are a few examples where objects have been gathered together in intriguing assemblages, a form of bricolage. There is the Waulkmill 'hoard', which contained glass and stone gaming pieces together with several more odd things including a miniature cauldron, an egg shaped stone, or amulet, and bangle fragments (see Hall forthcoming). The pits located in the floor of the Sollas wheelhouse, North Uist (Campbell 1991), contained interesting assemblages, one of which was covered by a quernstone, as was a pit in the structure at Burland in Shetland (Moore & Wilson 2014).

All these objects are most often described as toys or models in the archaeological literature, perhaps by comparison with modern dolls, though this is never made explicit. Sometimes they are interpreted as votive objects, miniature items standing in for the real thing in ritual contexts (see Hunter 2006). They are skeuomorphs — physical representations of one thing by another, in a different material.

Of all the gaming pieces I have examined very few can be described as skeuomorphs, or as miniatures. Most simply conform to a useful shape, one which is perhaps standard over a wide area, for example the simple hemispherical Tafl pieces, but which do not obviously represent other things. The Shetland Tafl pieces which I discussed in chapter 6 come close because they can be said to represent people or groups present in contemporary Iron Age society.

I discussed chess in terms of proxy action in chapter 2 and I believe these very awkward objects could be understood as proxy *objects*, which were designed to act as proxies for other things, and are thus deliberately, purposely, misleading. This is, I think, one difference between a skeuomorph and a representation: a representation does not attempt to mislead to the same extent. These miniature objects wear a mask — they cannot function as the real object does but are intended instead to play a role, to pretend to be what they are not. Their roles are given in a self-referential system very much like Huizinga's or Derrida's (1970) and in this way, then, they *are* playful and on this basis I could perhaps have considered them as gaming pieces. From Gregory Bateson's perspective (Bateson 1972) they are in fact the *most* playful kind of object: they are an example of Bateson's 'dog's nip' I mentioned in my introduction, in that they both are and are not the thing they represent.

The list of awkward objects goes on, and by the end of it I am no longer so sure that material culture actually conforms to the rather strict limitations put upon it by modern archaeologists. I get a sense too of humans as magpies, who like to gather strange or intriguing objects to themselves and are unwilling to let them go even when they have no use for them. When we gain control of these objects we create assemblages, which are rather like sets of gaming pieces. The places these objects are kept and used are important and help to provide meaning, just as gaming boards do for the pieces. We then assign relative value to the objects, and establish relationships between them, which can be manipulated in satisfying ways. The objects provide an endless supply of information about the world and are used by all of us, not only archaeologists, to think with. In the next chapter, my final discussion, I revisit the boundary between play and the world.

Chapter 8

Final Discussion

This study began by looking at people playing two different games in modern western society: chess, in Edinburgh and Orkney, and euchre, in Orkney. As part of this process it was the objects people played with, the cards and the chess pieces, and how people interacted with them, which really caught my attention.

In the case of chess this was partly due to the nature of the game itself: this is an activity which has its own fascinations and which encourages a kind of introspection where one does not look very far beyond the board. In the case of euchre, the cards served as a stepping off point for a wider look at the ways play was integrated into life and moved to the rhythms of a small Orcadian island.

I then turned to the archaeology and in doing so attempted to make use of what I had learned from chess and from euchre. I avoided any kind of direct ethnographic comparisons but instead sought to use those avenues of enquiry which I found productive when looking at modern games as 'ways in' to the more distant, archaeological, examples.

My response to chess and euchre was to examine the more cognitive aspects of play and to do so from an environmental perspective: I wanted to find out how people got along with the world and to explore how games might help me with this. For the archaeology, I also wanted to look at the same cognitive themes which had emerged and sought to do so by using case studies where I could place the play into its archaeological context.

Chess and Euchre

Chess and euchre are very different types of game and their differences were for me instructive and interesting. Chess is perhaps the ultimate game of strategy; it is a game for individuals which encourages planning and introspection. The game is open to all observers: by this I mean that there is no part of a game which is known only to one player(s). There is no element of chance. Players often come to the chess board with strategies, and tactics, prepared beforehand, and can rely on opportunities to put these learned skills into practice, even if their opponent will try their best to derail them.

Euchre is more of a team game and is less strategic. The players must deal with new situations as they occur, with only a guiding set of principles to help them. The game is social, chatty and inclusive. It incorporates a large element of chance. Each time the pack is shuffled new combinations are generated, and players must learn to cope with the results as they are worked out during the game. At the same time as playing to maximise their own score they must take account of their partner's and of their opponents' actions and potential actions.

Chess and euchre have much in common. They are both social activities if on different scales. It is the game which is important, whether chess or euchre, and they thus bring people together who might not otherwise meet. In doing so, they can cut across lines which might be drawn through society. Chess brought people from all over a city together, people who would not otherwise meet. In the case of euchre, this game took place in a small isolated community where most of the players knew one another or at least knew of them (or waved to them from a car/tractor while passing) but it still has a valuable role as a venue where old and young can meet and is one of the few places where locals and incomers can interact. I believe this is valuable in a small community which is changing rapidly. In a place where there is a tendency for individuals to socialise through pre-existing family networks, and through the church, going to euchre is an easy way for people to meet and expand their social circle.

The play provides a safe context for interaction – one which is governed by rules which determine where one may sit, whom one may talk with and so on. These are not onerous but part of the game and part of the experience; they are important because they provide a path for behaviour. If one is uncertain how to interact in an acceptable manner then the rules are there to remove uncertainty. The rules are not stifling, but during play they guide creativity in certain directions. The game is a kind of 'glue' which holds people together.

One thing which always struck me about chess clubs was how chess players nearly invariably asked what my rating was. Some players visibly lost interest when I told them I had no rating (in one chess club, at Edinburgh University, this reaction was so strong and so widespread that it put me off). There seemed to be a strong urge on the part of these players to place everyone into a kind of pecking order, one determined by an individual's proficiency. If the game is a form of culture, one can negotiate a place in it directly through the game and not by reference to any outside achievements.

One of the most interesting and problematic areas I found was the relationships between players and their gaming pieces, and this study reflects my various attempts to understand this: one question that had to be addressed was that of agency, and whether the pieces could be said to possess this in any way, albeit in Gell's secondary, lesser form.

My own solution followed the results of conversations with players – none ever spoke of the playing pieces in terms I could identify with an agency of objects, yet they were undeniably closely associated with the pieces during play; in a way, the players were forced to identify with their gaming pieces if the game was to work at all.

My solution, then, was to talk instead of action by proxy. This seemed to me to be a much more satisfying explanation, one which removed any need to assign agency to inert matter but which nonetheless included the pieces and cards within the scope of human action. This material aspect of play was very relevant to the archaeology, and it is one of the main themes which I looked for when I began that side of my study.

Archaeology and Play

When I turned towards the archaeology of play I became even more concerned with the material world; this is what archaeology must deal with, after all: soils, structures, *objects, things*. My aim here was to place the objects I encountered into some kind of context, a broader setting which would contribute a better sense of their meaning and significance.

Sometimes this context was chronological. Parallelopiped dice, for example, appear at a certain point in time during the Late Iron Age of Atlantic Scotland; knowing this allows for a better understanding of these small objects. In the case of Hnefetafl, the context of a single set was illuminating: the set of pieces from Scar Viking boat burial had a part to play in a highly charged event in the life of a community on a small Orcadian island.

One of the first problems I encountered when I turned to my archaeological case studies concerned the identification of play in the archaeological record. I had begun with a good idea that there were archaeological examples of play, and wanted to get to grips with these, yet I found that when I looked more carefully it became difficult to tell the difference between 'play things' and 'work things', for want of a better definition. The closer I looked, the more difficult I found it to tell the difference between say a parallelopiped dice, or a hnefetafl piece, and a cobble tool.

The reasons for this problem lay in the way play can be found everywhere, and particularly in its ambiguous relationship with ritual. I found many examples of seemingly utilitarian objects which had been used in playful ways, and playful objects deposited in seemingly very utilitarian contexts. I found entire sites whose location and function could as well be interpreted in terms of play as in any of the other more normal explanations favoured by archaeologists. Some gaming pieces, for example the small counters from Clickhimin Broch in Shetland, or the boards and pieces from Inchmarnock, had obviously been plucked from the surrounding environment (a beach), pressed into use and then abandoned. The affordance of the beach stones as gaming pieces came into focus for a short while and was then passed over in favour of something else, also long forgotten. It is lucky, and sometimes surprising, that these ephemeral uses could be recognised at all during excavation.

Ultimately, however, I resolved the quandary of how to recognise play in the archaeological record by focussing on those few examples which stood out for me as certain, well-defined. The problem did not go away but persisted in the background, however, and it is one of the factors which led to my final comments, below, which deal with the relationship between play and the world.

I also wanted to explore how an examination of the archaeological evidence for play could bring something more to what little is already known about these ancient societies. Play, as a topic, is more or less ignored in standard archaeological synthesis, probably for several reasons. It is undoubtedly seen by many archaeologists as 'not serious'; if one were to list the kinds of things which archaeologists are interested in and spend much of their time investigating, topics like 'economy' or 'landscape' or 'architecture' or 'social ranking' would undoubtedly sit at the top while play would lie somewhere near the bottom. This is because 'play' suffers from an association with 'leisure' — play is, for many, what takes place during leisure time, yet leisure is surely a modern concept, one which derives from a dialectical relationship with work. In the kinds of societies which were present in Atlantic Scotland during the first millennium AD it is by no means certain that there would have been such a hard and fast division between work and play and, in any case, the playful is ever present in our own modern western world, even if it is seldom acknowledged. Another reason why archaeologists might spend so little time with play is that it is (again, in our own modern western world) associated with children. Children are very seldom discussed in archaeological narratives — probably for similar reasons that women tend also to be ignored, and one could apply many of the arguments surrounding gender bias in archaeology to children (see Gilchrist 1999): children are seen as not economically active and are not considered to contribute to social life in a meaningful or long-lasting way; they therefore tend to be ignored. Archaeological pasts have too often been written by men, often with a colonial subtext (Thomas 2004), and these imagined pasts are very often serious places, populated by quite serious individuals engaged in 'subsistence activities' and seemingly very little else. My own response is that this link between play, games and children is more of a modern trope than any real long-term or fundamental aspect of human life. It is not difficult to find archaeological examples of play where the evidence clearly occurs in meaningful deposits, the kinds of context one does not necessarily associate with children. One only has to think of the Hnefetafl sets in Viking warrior graves, or mentioned in early Norse poetry, or the Lewis chess pieces, or the gaming pieces from high status La Tene graves... the list goes on. It is probably more difficult to find this kind of evidence where its context could reliably indicate that it is indeed part of children's play. The decorations on the slates from Inchmarnock, the writing in particular, were taken by the excavator to imply the presence of children here, yet the context is unusual; the site was ecclesiastical and seems to have functioned partly as a kind of 'school', a formal place of learning. The relationship between work, leisure and play is arguably even more complex in this kind of setting. The broader point to be made here is that there is no good evidence for a division between work and leisure in Iron Age Atlantic Scotland, in the terms with which we are familiar in our own society. Arguments which make use of the presence of gaming equipment to talk of children's lives run the risk of becoming circular if there is no additional evidence to make the case. Games were not only played by children; play was and is ever present, it quietly lurks below the surface of daily life.

If this study of the archaeology of play brought home to me how intertwined it was with daily life, it also pointed up how objects are used to think with. It was clear to me that the players were forced to follow the events on the chess board, or euchre table and could not rely on any internal model. Playing the game was, for the players, about discovering what was happening there before them, in the moment. This aspect of play was also highlighted in chess and euchre; for me this was one of the most interesting things about play and it was something which I looked for in the archaeology. If I had not carried out my fieldwork with euchre players and even more particularly with chess players, I do not think I would have been alerted to this aspect of play.

The clearest example of this type of relationship which I could find in the archaeological record was probably with the parallelopiped dice, if only because of their function as random number generators, which introduced an element of chance much as shuffling the deck of cards did for euchre. The parallelopiped dice were difficult to analyse because I immediately became embroiled in questions surrounding the relationship between play and ritual/divination, yet they were interesting and rewarding because of this and I could see how the uses of the dice entailed a kind of following, for example as seen in their use and deposition after conflagration.

The archaeology also informed the ethnography so that this was not a one-way relationship but a reflexive one. When I looked at the archaeology, the material relationships came to the fore, and were so clearly important that this in turn influenced the ways I approached the ethnography: I began to look for the ways the players used the playing pieces as objects, not just as gaming pieces.

Revisiting Huizinga

One of the most striking elements to this study, for me, has been the difficulty I have found in attempting to draw a clear dividing line between play and daily life. This was most marked with the archaeology, and in Chapter 7 I discussed some of the awkward objects I encountered, objects which I found particularly difficult to pin down as play things. I found this problem surprising because I was following a standard definition of play, one which has been accepted for over half a century and which emphasises a separation between play and the real world in which it is enveloped. Of all the examples of play which I studied, Chess at the Edinburgh Chess Club conformed best to this norm, probably a reflection of the club's location in a city, and of the fact that it owns its own premises. The Edinburgh Chess Club is effectively set apart from much that goes on around it, and populated by individuals who do not know one another outside of chess. They do not have to mix or compromise with the outside world while at play. The chess is thus cushioned or wrapped in several layers of separation before a game even begins; it is set apart in time (meetings take place in the evenings, after work hours) and place.

With euchre, I could see that the game was well-defined yet inextricably bound up with the wider Westray society. When it came to the archaeology, I could find some very clear examples of play, which were interesting in their own right and helped me to understand much more about play, yet I could find more which were ambiguous and which pointed towards other ways of understanding the relationship between play and daily life. There was obviously a problem here with my model for play; this was fundamentally based on Johan Huizinga (1955), and so it is worthwhile revisiting his theories.

When Huizinga published *Homo Ludens*, more than seventy years ago, he set the tone of play enquiry for nearly every subsequent scholar down to the present day, even if much of the body of the book is now in need of a re-assessment. He did this by setting out some definitions for play, which I listed in my introduction; they are simple and so make play likewise appear to be straightforward, well-defined. This was his greatest contribution, I believe: he presented a way by which play could be recognised, even if the content was more difficult to understand.

Huizinga based his definition on an understanding of rules as limiting factors. The behaviour which constitutes play is bounded by these rules and each of the many varieties of play has its own particular set. For Huizinga, the rules set play apart from daily life; they form a well-defined boundary within which play takes place.

However, when viewed from this perspective, almost all activities can be said to be governed by rules: shopping and eating, or driving, for example. Most activities presuppose some attention to specific rules of behaviour, and could be viewed as taking place in a kind of bubble: as with play, they have a well-defined beginning and end, and specific ways of behaving during the activity, which have been agreed beforehand with other participants. Are these also examples of play? They might seem to lack the element of uncertain outcome, which is usually thought of as essential to play, yet there is uncertainty in our daily interaction with the world.

The problem here is not so much that Huizinga's definitions were vague but has to do with his concept of rules and rule-bound behaviour. In the process of carrying out this study I came to a different view of rules, one which was based on my experiences with the people who play chess and euchre but also with the process of archaeology.

When I visited the Westray euchre club for the first time I did not know the rules; I could not play the game, yet a kindly person took the time to explain them to me. It is interesting that, though I did not realise just then, I was not told all of them at once. I was given the bare essentials – enough to get me started, and in any case many of the rules are shared with other card games, so it is possible to get along for a little while. Huizinga would have argued, I think, that these rules, as they were given to me, formed the boundary to euchre. By attending to them I colluded with other players in the formation of the play, which continued until we were all satisfied that enough euchre had been played for one night. The rules also provided for an end point to the play. I would argue that there is another way to understand them, however. They should be seen not as boundaries which must be respected but rather as paths and signposts which run through the game and which must be followed. One rule leads on to others, which is why I was not told them all; in some games of euchre not all of the rules are encountered, and there was always someone else there to help out if an unexpected fork in the path was ahead. In this sense the rules can be seen as lines, every rule being one of Ingold's 'entangled lines of life, growth and movement' (Ingold 2011, 63). From this perspective the game is not as set apart as it seems, and some of the rules for euchre are so similar to ways of living on the island that I could follow it outside on to the farms.

One of the attractions of Huizinga's approach, historically, has been that it has allowed play to be understood in isolation. It has also, unfortunately, allowed the subject to be side-lined. Those who are interested in play have made repeated pleas that it not be marginalised, and then lamented that this has been its fate (see Callois 2001[1958], Hendry & Raveri 2002, Bornet & Burger 2012). Victor Turner deserves a special mention as someone who sought to place play in a central position in daily life, but modern engagement with play theory now revolves mostly around sport, theatre, and performance (Schechner 2002). Other play forms, and the relationship between play and 'real life', are more rarely studied.

Huizinga's definitions allowed some (most famously Geertz, 1993) to see play as an activity which is so set apart as to be irrelevant to society as a whole. If the events which took place during play did so within such a firm boundary, formed by its own peculiar rules, it was possible for play, including all of its fascinating and varied forms, to be squeezed into a box labelled 'play' and then to be ignored, or side-lined. This is unhelpful and has been due to a particular understanding of the rules which govern play, where they are envisaged as the boundaries to the bubble, limiting factors which constrain creativity. My own experience of chess and euchre showed how the game is instead permeated by the rules, many of which are only encountered as one works one's way through the play, and how the rules encourage creativity.

At the same time that Huizinga emphasised play's boundaries, however, he coined the term 'ludic' as a more general adjective to apply to the 'playful':

> '...ethnology and related disciplines give too little place to the notion of play. For me, at any rate, the commonly used terminology with respect to play was not sufficient. I constantly felt the need for an adjective to *play*, that simply expresses 'what belongs to play or playing'. 'Playful' would not do, as it has too special a nuance of meaning. I should like to be permitted, therefore, to introduce the word *ludic*. Although the presumed basic form is unknown in Latin, in French the word is found as *ludique* in psychological tracts.' (extract taken from Van Bremen 2002, 220, emphasis in original. This passage is not given in the English translation but is in the Dutch version).

There seems to be a contradiction here: If play is so tightly bounded and set apart how can it be that it seems to 'leak' into all other aspects of our lives? Huizinga also acknowledged the challenges inherent in studying play and he pointed out the difficulties of distinguishing it from other elements of social life. He noted, for example, how difficult it was to separate play from ritual and also gave examples where play was so serious that participation could be dangerous, even life threatening (Caillois' categorisations of play recognised this strand, specifically terming it 'agon').

In part, Huizinga seems to have resolved this contradiction by taking each game as a particular instance of play. This, however, still leaves us with problems of definition: what is a 'game', and what is the difference between a game and play more generally? Games seem to be easy: they conform to Huizinga's definitions – chess is a game, as is euchre, and hnefetafl. What, then, is play? There are very many meanings of the word (Huizinga devotes an entire chapter to an exploration of the etymology) but rather than seek a linguistic answer I would like to examine play as an activity and look at what people do when they play. My answer, it must be admitted, is somewhat circular because in wishing to find out what play is I have returned to games: if a game is a particular instance of something more general, then any one game should contain elements of the whole. If enough games are examined then a complete answer should be arrived at.

For myself, the key to the puzzle of the nature of the relationship between play and real life can be found in the player's relationships with the artefacts they play with. I do not believe that there is in fact a boundary between play and daily life. Particular instances of play – games - arise at particular times and places, are briefly concrete, and then fade away again. The use of beach pebbles at Inchmarnock, or pottery sherds at Clickhimin, as gaming pieces, makes me think of this: the objects are quickly co-opted into play, then set aside as easily. This is why play is so difficult to find; for much of the time, I believe, play is in fact ubiquitous in the many small ways in which we encounter the world around us.

Playing with things

One of the features that struck me about the way people played chess was the way they held their chess pieces. Very often a player would move a piece, but when it was on the new square they would not let it go but hold on to it. Sometimes they would then move the piece to another square, or yet another, or put it back where it had been and move another piece instead. There is a rule, I think an informal one which is not always observed, whereby a player is not considered to have made their move until they have released their hold on the piece. At euchre, too, there were occasions where a player put down a card but then snatched it up again without releasing it. Always this was done quickly, partly because the next player would play very soon but also because there is a commonly agreed, informal, length of time beyond which the move is considered final. If one plays a card, one needs to retract it pretty quickly or the other players will consider it done. What was going on here? On the one hand it seemed to be quite simple: a player had made a mistake or had changed his or her mind, and this is what I was told when I queried players about this. Sometimes a chess player was doing something different, and would admit that they were not in fact sure about a given move and needed to see the piece there, in its new location, before they committed themselves. This was all much as I had expected. I have played chess myself for many years and know that I cannot always predict how the movement of a piece will change the pattern on the board until it is physically there in front of me. The rule about letting go of the piece allows for the players to experiment a little before they commit.

On the one hand this seemed to be very reasonable. Much is made of the complexity of chess: there are more potential moves available on a chess board than there are electrons in the universe (mathematically true, see Binmore 2007, 37), so obviously a player cannot hold all of this in his or her head and must instead feel their way through the options. Yet in any situation, and even given that most players think two or perhaps three moves ahead, there are usually only a few real alternatives and most possibilities are in fact clearly bad choices. Also, this fearsome complexity derives from a mere 32 pieces on an 8x8 grid of cells. How much more complex and difficult to take account of is a forest? Or a room full of people? The point I am trying to make is that the game is not always as complex as it seems, even if the maths make it appear so. Given this, why do the players need to see the pieces on the board before they move? In Chapter 2, I made the point that the players behave as if they are thinking with the pieces; they are involved in an active engagement with these objects whereby thought is 'ratcheted' forward in step with the pieces. They may think ahead of the pieces as they are on the board, but they are also being continually pulled back to take account of the way they are now. This behaviour is not a response to an overly complicated system, but just the way people deal with the world. The players deal with what they need to at that moment in time and let the rest stay out there until they are ready to deal with it.

Taking all these observations into account, how can the study of play contribute to the debate surrounding cognition? Recall the question posed by Clark & Chalmers: 'Where does the mind stop and the rest of the world begin?' (Clark & Chalmers 2010 [1998], 27). Suppose we take this question but substitute 'play' for 'mind': where does *play* stop and the rest of the world begin? My answer to this is that there is no boundary between play and the world. I have shown that the relationship between mind and world is dynamic, fluid and mutable. Play offers a basis for understanding this relationship.

Play, as I have encountered it, revolves around the manipulation of objects. Admittedly, this is not the case for all play and I could not always separate the ludic use of objects from any other kind. At the same time as players use objects to play with, they think with them too. Hutchins (1995, 280-283) talks of social scaffolding, and Clark (1998, 45-47, following Vygotsky) of the use of the environment (his example is spice racks). The game, especially the pieces, scaffolds thought too. One of the ways it does this is by ratcheting thought backwards and forwards in step with the play.

A game also brings objects together in new and continually changing ways. This is bricolage, or the kaleidoscope (Ingold 2007), and again it is cognitive, yet I cannot see how it is unique to play. This kaleidoscope is full of uncertain outcomes, which is part of its charm and why it must be followed, diligently, by the participants. We never know completely how our understanding of the world will be altered by these new constellations of objects.

Games fascinate not only because they are particular instances of play but also because they are simplified, codified, instances of real life, and this brings me full circle back to Huizinga, who claimed that culture arises in the form of play. I now find myself agreeing with the spirit of his statement, even if he made it in the context of a poorly understood concept of culture. I now believe that the manner in which we interact with the world is fundamentally playful, or ludic, and that everything else follows from this.

References

Alexander, C. H. O'D. 1972. *Fischer v. Spassky. Reykjavik 1972*. London: Penguin.

Ambers, J. 2010. Scientific Analysis of Painted Quartz Pebbles. In *Excavations at Old Scatness, Shetland Volume 1: The Pictish Village and Viking Settlement*, eds. S. J. Dockrill, J. M. Bond, V. E. Turner, L. D. Brown, D. J. Bashford, J. E. Cussans and R. A. Nicholson. Lerwick: Shetland Heritage Publications, pp. 322-323.

Arbman, H. 1943. Birka Untersuchingen und Studien I: Die Gräber. Stockholm: Almquist and Wiksell, Vol 1.

Armit, I. 1990. Introduction. In *Beyond the Brochs: changing perspectives in the Scottish Atlantic Iron Age*, ed. I. Armit. Edinburgh: Edinburgh University Press, pp. 1-4.

Armit, I. 1997. *Celtic Scotland*. London: Batsford.

Armit, I. 2005a. The Atlantic Roundhouse: a Beginner's Guide. In *Tall Stories? 2 Millennia of Brochs*, eds. V. E. Turner, S. J. Dockrill, R. A. Nicholson and J. M. Bond. Lerwick: Shetland Amenity Trust, pp. 5-10.

Armit, I. 2005b. Land-Holding and Inheritance in the Atlantic Scottish Iron Age. In *Tall Stories? 2 Millennia of Brochs*, eds. V. E. Turner, S. J. Dockrill, R. A. Nicholson and J. M. Bond. Lerwick: Shetland Amenity Trust, pp. 129-143.

Armit, I. 2006. *Anatomy of an Iron Age Roundhouse: The Cnip Wheelhouse Excavations, Lewis*. Edinburgh: Society of Antiquaries of Scotland Monograph.

Ballin Smith, B. ed. 1994. *Howe: Four Millennia of Orkney Prehistory, Excavation 1978-82*. Edinburgh: Society of Antiquaries of Scotland Monograph 9.

Barrett, J. C. 2000. A Thesis on Agency. In *Agency in Archaeology*, eds. M-A. Dobres, and J. Robb. London: Routledge, pp. 61-68.

Barrett, J. C. and S. M. Foster 1991. Passing the time in Iron Age Scotland. In *Scottish Archaeology: New Perceptions*, eds. W. S. Hanson and E. A. Slater. Aberdeen: Aberdeen University Press.

Bartlett, F. C. 1995 [1932]. *Remembering*. Cambridge: Cambridge University Press.

Bateson, G. 1972. *Steps to an Ecology of Mind*. New York: Ballantine Books.

Becker, A. 2007. The Royal Game of Ur. In *Ancient Board Games in Perspective*, ed. I. Finkel. London: British Museum Publications, pp. 11-15.

Bell, C 1992. *Ritual Theory, Ritual Practice*. New York: Oxford University Press.

Bergson, A. 1911. *Creative Evolution* (trans. A. Mitchell). London: Macmillan.

Binmore, K. 2007. *Game Theory: A Very Short Introduction*. Oxford: Oxford University Press.

Bond, J. 2003. A Growing Success? Agricultural Intensification and Risk Management in Late Iron Age Orkney. In *Sea Change: Orkney and Northern Europe in the Later Iron Age AD300-800*, eds. J. Downes, and A. Ritchie. Brechin: Pinkfoot Press, pp. 105-110.

Bornet, P. and M. Burger 2012 eds. *Religions in Play: Games, Rituals, and Virtual Worlds*. Zurich: Pano Verlag.

Bradley, R. 1998. *The Passage of Arms*. Oxford: Oxbow Books.

Bronkhorst, J. 2012. Can there be Play in Ritual? Reflections on the Nature of Ritual. In *Religions in Play: Games, Rituals, and Virtual Worlds* eds. P. Bornet and M. Burger. Zurich: Pano Verlag, pp. 161-175.

Burton, R. J. F. 2004. Reconceptualising the 'Behavioural Approach' in Agricultural Studies: a Socio-psychological Perspective. *Journal of Rural Studies* 20: 359-371.

Caillois, R. 2001 [1958]. *Man, Play and Games*, trans. Meyer Barash. New York: Free Press.

Campbell, E. 1991. The Excavations of a Wheelhouse and Other Iron Age Structures at Sollas, North Uist, by RJC Atkinson in 1957. *Proceedings of the Society of Antiquaries of Scotland* 121: 117-173.

Caplan, P. 2000. Introduction: Risk Revisited. In *Risk Revisited*, ed. P. Caplan. London: Pluto Press.

Chapman, J. 2000. *Fragmentation in Archaeology*. London: Routledge.

Chase, W. G. and H. A. Simon 1973. Perception in chess. *Cognitive Psychology* 4: 55-81.

Childe, V. G. 1925. *The Dawn of European Civilization*. London: Kegan Paul.

Childe, V. G. 1931. *Skara Brae: A Pictish Village in Orkney*. London: Kegan Paul.

Childe, V. G. 1935. *Prehistory of Scotland*. London: Kegan Paul.

Clark, A. 1989. *Microcognition: Philosophy, Cognitive Science and Parallel Distributive Processing*. Cambridge, Mass: MIT Press.

Clark, A. 1998. *Being There. Putting Brain, Body, and World Together Again*. Cambridge, Mass: MIT Press.

Clark, A. and D. J. Chalmers 2010. The Extended Mind. In *The Extended Mind*, ed. R. Menary. Cambridge, Mass: MIT Press, pp. 27-42. Originally published in *Analysis* 58 (1998): 10-23.

Clarke, D. V. 1970. Bone Dice and the Scottish Iron Age. *Proceedings of the Prehistoric Society* 36: 214-232.

Clarke, D. V., T. Cowie and A. Foxon 1985. *Symbols of Power at the Time of Stonehenge*. Edinburgh: National Museum of Antiquities of Scotland.

Close-Brooks, J. 1986. Excavations at Clatchard Craig, Fife. *Proceedings of the Society of Antiquaries of Scotland* 116: 117-184.

Conneller, C. 2011. *An Archaeology of Materials*. London: Routledge.

Connerton, P. 1989. *How Societies Remember*. Cambridge: Cambridge University Press.

Crawford, B. 1987. *Scandinavian Scotland*. Leicester: Leicester University Press.

Crone, A. and E. Campbell 2005. *A Crannog of the 1 Millennium AD*. Edinburgh: Society of Antiquaries of Scotland Monograph.

Crowe, D. W. and D. K. Washburn 2004 eds. *Symmetry Comes of Age: the Role of Pattern in Culture*. Washington: University of Washington Press.

Culin, S. 1975 [1907]. *Games of the North American Indians*. New York: Dover Publications Inc.

Curle, C. L. 1982. *Pictish and Norse Finds from the Brough of Birsay 1934-74*. Edinburgh: Society of Antiquaries of Scotland Monograph 1.

Davidson, J. L. and A. S. Henshall 1989. *The Chambered Cairns of Orkney*. Edinburgh: Edinburgh University Press.

Derevenski, J. S. 2000. Material Culture Shock: Confronting Expectations in the Material Culture of Children. In *Children and Material Culture*, ed. J. S. Derevenski. London: Routledge, pp. 1-16.

Derevenski, J. S. 2000a ed. *Children and Material Culture*. London: Routledge.

Derrida, J. 1970. Structure, Sign, and Play in the Discourse of the Human Sciences. In *The Languages of Criticism and the Sciences of Man*, eds R. Macksey, and E. Donato. Baltimore: John Hopkins Press, pp. 247-272.

De Voogt, A. 2012. Mancala at the Pyramids of Meroe. *Antiquity* 86 (334): 1155-1166.

Dobres, M-A. and J. Robb 2000 eds. *Agency in Archaeology*. London: Routledge.

Dockrill, S. J., J. M. Bond, V. E. Turner, L. D. Brown, D. J. Bashford, J. E. Cussans, and R. A. Nicholson 2010 eds. *Excavations at Old Scatness, Shetland Volume 1: The Pictish Village and Viking Settlement.* Lerwick: Shetland Heritage Publications.

Dockrill, S. J., J. M. Bond, V. E. Turner, L. D. Brown, D. J. Bashford, J. E. Cussans, and R. A. Nicholson 2015 eds. *Excavations at Old Scatness, Shetland Volume 2: The Broch and Iron Age Village.* Lerwick: Shetland Heritage Publications.

Donald, M. 1991. *Origins of the Modern Mind.* Harvard: Harvard University Press.

Douglas, M. 1992. *Risk and Blame.* London: Routledge.

Eales, R. 2007. Changing Cultures: The Reception of Chess into Western Europe in the Middle Ages. In *Ancient Board Games in Perspective* ed. I. L. Finkel. London: British Museum Publications, pp. 162-168.

Edwards, K. and I. Ralston 2003. eds *Scotland After the Ice Age: Environment, Archaeology and History, 8000BC-AD1000.* Edinburgh: Edinburgh University Press.

Finkel, I. 2007. On the Rules for the Royal Game of Ur. In *Ancient Board Games in Perspective,* ed. I. Finkel. London: British Museum Publications, pp. 16-32.

Fojut, N. 1982a. Towards a Geography of Shetland Brochs. *Glasgow Archaeological Journal* 9: 38-59.

Fojut, N. 1982b. Is Mousa a Broch? *Proceedings of the society of Antiquaries of Scotland* 111: 220-28.

Foster, S. 1989. Analysis of Special Patterns in Buildings (Access Analysis) as an Insight into Social Structure: Examples from the Scottish Atlantic Iron Age. *Antiquity* 63: 40-50.

Foster, S. M. 1990. Pins, Combs and the Chronology of Later Atlantic Iron Age Settlement. In *Beyond the Brochs,* ed. I. Armit. Edinburgh: Edinburgh University Press, pp. 143-174.

Geertz, C. 1980. *Negara: The Theatre State in Nineteenth-Century Bali.* Princeton: Princeton University Press.

Geertz, C. 1993 [1973]. *The Interpretation of Cultures.* Illinois: Fontana Press.

Gell, A. 1998. *Art and Agency: An Anthropological Theory.* Oxford: Clarendon Press.

Gibson, J. J. 1979. *The Ecological Approach to Visual Perception.* Boston: Houghton Mifflin.

Giddens, A. 1984. *The Constitution of Society.* Cambridge: Polity Press.

Gilchrist, R. 1999. *Gender and Archaeology: Contesting the Past.* London: Routledge.

Ginn, V. and S. Rathbone 2012. *Corrstown: A Coastal Community. Excavations of a Bronze Age Village in Northern Ireland.* Oxford: Oxbow books.

Giulianotti, R. 2004 ed. *Sport and Modern Social Theorists.* London: Palgrave Macmillan.

Gobet, F., A. de Voogt and J. Retschitzki 2004. *Moves in Mind. The Psychology of Board Games.* New York: Psychology Press.

Gosden, C. 1994. *Social Being and Time.* New Jersey: John Wiley & Sons.

Graham-Campbell, J. and C. E. Batey 1998. *Vikings in Scotland. An Archaeological Survey.* Edinburgh: Edinburgh University Press.

Grant, M. 2000. *Gladiators.* London: Penguin.

Guttman, A. 1994. *Games and Empires.* Columbia: Columbia University Press.

Hall, M. 2007. *Playtime in Pictland: The Material Culture of Gaming in Early Medieval Scotland.* Rosemarkie: Groam House Museum.

Hall, M. *forthcoming.* The Waulkmill Gaming Counters: Discovery and Gaming Context. In *The Use and Reuse of Stone Circles. Fieldwork at Five Scottish Monuments and its Implications,* eds. Bradley, R. and C. Nimura. Unpublished Manuscript.

Hamilton, J. R. C. 1956. *Excavations at Jarlshof, Shetland*. Edinburgh: HMSO.

Hamilton, J. R. C. 1968 *Excavations at Clickhimin, Shetland*. Edinburgh: HMSO.

Harding, D. W. and I. Armit 1990. Survey and Excavation in West Lewis. In *Beyond the Brochs: changing perspectives in the Atlantic Iron Age,* ed. I. Armit. Edinburgh: Edinburgh University Press, pp. 71-107.

Harding, D. W. and P. G. Topping 1986. *Callanish Archaeological Research Centre 1 Annual Report*. Edinburgh: Department of Archaeology, University of Edinburgh.

Hedges, J. W. 1987. *Bu, Gurness and the Brochs of Orkney*. Oxford: British Archaeological Reports (British Series) 163, 164, 165. Three Vols.

Henderson, G. and I. Henderson 2004. *The Art of the Picts. Sculpture and Metalwork in Early Medieval Scotland*. London: Thames and Hudson.

Hendry, J. and M. Raveri 2002 eds. *Japan at Play: the Ludic and Logic of Power*. London: Routledge.

Hill, J. D. 1995. *Ritual and Rubbish in the Iron Age of Wessex*. Oxford: British Archaeological Reports (British Series) 242.

Hingley, R. 1992. Society in Scotland from 700 BC to AD 200. *Proceedings of the Society of Antiquaries of Scotland* 122: 7-53.

Hingley, R., H. Moore, J. E. Triscott and G. Wilson 1997. The Excavation of Two Later Iron Age Fortified Homesteads at Aldclune, Blair Atholl, Perth & Kinross. *Proceedings of the Society of Antiquaries of Scotland* 127: 407-466.

Hirst, W. and D. Gluck 1999. Revisiting John Dean's Memory. In *Ecological Approaches to Cognition: Essays in Honour of Ulric Neisser,* eds. E. Winograd, R. Fivush, and W. Hirst. London: Laurence Erlbaum Associates, Emory Symposia in Cognition., pp. 253-284.

Hodder, I. 2012. *Entangled: An Archaeology of the Relationships between Humans and Things*. New Jersey: Wiley-Blackwell.

Huizinga, J. 1955 [1950]. *Homo Ludens: a Study of the Play Element in Culture*. Boston: Beacon Press.

Hunter, F. 2006. Miniature Objects. In *Anatomy of an Iron Age Roundhouse: The Cnip Wheelhouse Excavations, Lewis,* ed. I. Armit. 2006. Edinburgh: Society of Antiquaries of Scotland monograph, pp. 150-151.

Hunter, J. 2007. *Investigations in Sanday Orkney: Vol 1, Excavations at Pool, Sanday*. Kirkwall: Orcadian publications.

Hunter, J. 1986. *Rescue Excavations at the Brough of Birsay 1974-1982*. Edinburgh: Society of Antiquaries of Scotland monograph 4.

Hunter, J. 1997. The Landberg, Fair Isle (Dunrossness parish), Iron Age promontory fort. In *Discovery & Excavation in Scotland*. Edinburgh: Royal Commission on Ancient and Historical Monuments of Scotland, pp 68-69.

Hutchins, E. 1995. *Cognition in the Wild*. Cambridge, Mass.: MIT Press.

Hurcombe, L. M. 2014. *Perishable Material Culture in Prehistory: Investigating the missing majority*. London: Routledge.

Hyman Jr, I. E. 1999. Creating False Autobiographical Memories: Why People Believe Their Memory Errors. In *Ecological Approaches to Cognition: Essays in Honour of Ulric Neisser*, eds E. Winograd, R. Fivush and W. Hirst. London: Laurence Erlbaum Associates, Emory Symposia in Cognition., pp. 229-252.

Ilberry, B. W. 1978. Agricultural Decision-making: a Behavioural Perspective. *Progress in Human Geography* l2 (3): 448-466.

Ingold, T. 2000. *The Perception of the Environment*. London: Routledge.

Ingold, T. 2007. *Lines: A Brief History*. London: Routledge.

Ingold, T. 2007a. Introduction to Part 1. In *Creativity and Cultural Improvisation,* eds E. Hallam, and T. Ingold. ASA Monograph 44. Oxford: Berg, pp. 45-54.

Ingold, T. 2011. *Being Alive. Essays on Movement Knowledge and Description.* London: Routledge.

Ingold, T. 2013. *Making. Anthropology, Archaeology, Art and Architecture.* London: Routledge.

Ingold, T. and E. Hallam 2007. Creativity and Cultural Improvisation: An Introduction. In *Creativity and Cultural Improvisation,* eds. E. Hallam and T. Ingold. ASA Monograph 44. Oxford: Berg, pp. 1-24.

Jackson, K. H. 1971 [1951]. *A Celtic Miscellany.* London: Penguin.

Jones, G. and T. Jones 1998 [1949]. *The Mabinogion.* London: Everyman Library.

Joyce, R. and J. Pollard 2010. Archaeological Assemblages and Practices of Deposition. In *The Oxford handbook of Material culture studies, eds.* D. Hicks and M. C. Beaudry. Oxford: Oxford University Press, pp. 291-312.

Junod, H. A. 1927. *The Life of a South African Tribe.* London: Macmillan & Co. 2 vols.

Kaland, S. H. H. 1993. The Settlement of Westness, Rousay. In The Viking age in Caithness, Orkney and the North Atlantic, eds. C. E. Batey, J. Jesch and C. D. Morris. Edinburgh: Edinburgh University Press, pp. 312-317.

Keller, J. and C. Keller 1991. 'Thinking and Acting with Iron' Beckman Institute Cognitive Science Technical Reports Cs-91-08, Champaign-Urbana, Ill.: Beckman Institute.

Kilpatrick, K. A. 2011. The Iconography of the Papil Stone: Sculptural and Literary Comparisons with a Pictish motif. *Proceedings of the Society of Antiquaries of Scotland* 141: 159-205.

Kirsch, D. 1995. The Intelligent Use of Space. *Artificial Intelligence* 73: 31-68.

Knappett, C. 2005. *Thinking Through Material Culture.* Philadelphia: University of Pennsylvania Press.

Lamb, R. G. 1980 *Iron Age Promontory Forts in the Northern Isles.* Oxford: British Archaeological Reports (British Series) 79.

Lamb, R. G. 1995. Papil, Picts and Papar. In *Northern Isles Connections,* ed. B. E. Crawford. Kirkwall: The Orkney Press, pp. 9-28.

Lane, A. 1987. English Migrants in the Hebrides: Atlantic Scotland B revisited. *Proceedings of the Society of Antiquaries of Scotland* 117: 47-66.

Latour, B. 1999. *Pandora's Hope. Essays on the reality of science studies.* Cambridge, Mass.: Harvard University Press

Lévi-Strauss, C. 1966. *The Savage Mind.* Chicago: The University of Chicago Press.

Lawrence, D. 2005. An Anthropomorphic Carving from Pictish Orkney. *Proceedings of the Society of Antiquaries of Scotland* 135: 309-318.

Linnaeus, C. 1811. *Lachesis Lapponica or A Tour in Lappland.* Vol 2. Available online at https://archive.org/details/lachesislapponic01linn accessed on 3/1/16.

Lowe, C. 2008. *Inchmarnock: An Early Historic Island Monastery and its Archaeological Landscape.* Edinburgh: Society of Antiquaries of Scotland Monograph.

Loy, J. W. and G. S. Kenyon 1969. *Sport, Culture and Society.* London: Macmillan.

MacGregor, A. 1974. The Broch of Burrian, North Ronaldsay, Orkney. *Proceedings of the Society of Antiquaries of Scotland* 105: 63-118.

MacGregor, A. 1985. *Bone, Antler Ivory and Horn: The Technology of Skeletal Materials Since the Roman Period.* London: Croom Helm.

Mackie, E. W. 1970. The Scottish Iron Age. *Scottish Historical Review* 49: 1-32.

Mackie, E. W. 2002. *The Roundhouses, Brochs and Wheelhouses of Atlantic Scotland c.700 BC-AD 500. Architecture and Material Culture. Part 1, The Orkney and Shetland Isles.* Oxford: British Archaeological Reports (British Series) 342.

Malafouris, L. 2013. *How Things Shape the Mind. A Theory of Material Engagement.* Cambridge, Mass.: MIT Press.

Malafouris, L. and C. Renfrew 2010 eds *The Cognitive Life of Things.* Cambridge: McDonald Institute Monograph.

Mark, M. 2007. The Beginnings of Chess. In *Ancient Board Games in Perspective,* ed. I. L. Finkel. London: British Museum Publications, pp. 138-157.

Mauss, M. 2007. *The Manual of Ethnography.* New York: Berghahn Books.

McClymond, K. 2012. Introduction: Relating Play and Ritual. In *Religions in Play: Games, Rituals, and Virtual Worlds,* eds. P. Bornet and M. Burger. Zurich: Pano Verlag, pp. 155-160.

McCullagh, R. P. J. and R. Tipping 1998. *The Lairg Project 1988-1996: The Evolution of an Archaeological Landscape in Northern Scotland.* Edinburgh: STAR Monograph 3.

Meehan, C. H. W. 1862. *The Law and Practice of the Game of Euchre, by a Professor.* Philadelphia: TB Peterson and Brothers.

Menary, R. 2010 ed.. *The Extended Mind.* Cambridge, Mass.: MIT Press.

Miller, D. 2005 ed. *Materiality.* Durham, N.C.: Duke University Press.

Mithen, S. J. 1996. *The Prehistory of the Mind.* London: Thames & Hudson.

Moore, H. and G. Wilson 2006-2013. *Excavations at Links of Noltland, Westray, Orkney: Data Structure Reports.* Edinburgh: Unpublished reports for Historic Environment Scotland.

Moore, H. and G. Wilson 2011a. *Shifting Sands. Links of Noltland, Westray: Interim Report on Neolithic and Bronze Age Excavations 2007-09.* Historic Scotland Monograph.

Moore, H. and G. Wilson 2011b. *Knowe of Skea: DSR 2000-2009.* Unpublished report.

Moore, H. and G. Wilson 2014. *Ebbing Shores: Survey and Excavation of Coastal Archaeology in Shetland 1995-2008.* Historic Scotland Monograph.

Moore, H. and G. Wilson forthcoming. *Excavation of an Iron Age Settlement, Souterrain and Viking long house at Langskaill Souterrain, Westray, Orkney.*

Morris, C. D. 1989. *The Birsay Bay Project: Coastal Sites Beside the Brough Road, Birsay, Orkney: excavations 1976-1982.* Durham: University of Durham Dept. of Archaeology, Monograph Series No.1.

Muir, E. 1997. *Ritual in Early Modern Europe.* Cambridge: Cambridge University Press.

Murray, H. R. J. 1913. *A History of Chess.* Oxford: Oxford University Press.

Murray, H. R. J. 1952. *A History of Board Games Other Than Chess.* Oxford: Oxford University Press.

Mykura, W. 1976. *Orkney and Shetland (British Regional Geology).* Edinburgh: British Geological Survey, HMSO.

Neisser, U. 2009. Memory with a Grain of Salt. In *Memory: An Anthology,* eds. Wood, H. H. and A. S. Byatt. London: Vintage, pp. 80-88.

Neisser, U. and R. Fivush 1994 eds *The Remembering Self: Construction and Accuracy in the Self-narrative.* Emory Symposia in Cognition 6. Cambridge: Cambridge University Press.

Olson, B. 2010. *In defence of things: Archaeology and the Ontology of Objects.* Lanham MD: AltaMira Press

Owen, O. A. and M. Dalland 1999. *Scar: A Viking Boat Burial on Sanday, Orkney*. Fife: Tuckwell Press.

Olwig, K. 2008. Performing on the Landscape Versus Doing Landscape. In *Ways of Walking: Ethnography and Practice on Foot*, eds. T. Ingold and J. Lee Vergunst. Farnham: Ashgate Press, pp. 81-92.

Ovrevik, S. 1990 [1985]. The Second Millennium BC and After. In *The Prehistory of Orkney*, ed. C. Renfrew. Edinburgh: Edinburgh University Press, pp. 131-149.

Page, R. I. 1995. *Chronicles of the Vikings*. London: British Museum Press.

Palsson, H. 1996. *Voluspa: The Sybil's Prophecy*. Edinburgh: Lockharton Press.

Parker Pearson, M. 1999. *The Archaeology of Death and Burial*. London: Sutton Publishing Ltd.

Parker Pearson, M. and M. Zvelebil 2014 *Excavations at Cill Donnain: A Bronze Age Settlement and Iron Age Wheelhouse in South Uist*. Oxford: Oxbow Books.

Parlett, D. 1999. *The Oxford History of Board Games*. Oxford: Oxford University Press.

Parlett, D. 2004. *The Oxford A-Z of Card Games*. Oxford: Oxford University Press.

Parlett, D. 2013. *Historic Card Games: Euchre*. http://www.davidparlett.co.uk/histocs/euchre.html. (Accessed 30/11/13)

Pearson, M. and M. Shanks 2001. *Theatre/Archaeology*. London: Routledge.

Philidor, A. D. 1820. Analyse du jeu des Echecs. France.

Piaget, J. 1962. *Play Dreams and Imitation in Childhood*. London: Routledge.

Piggott, S. 1966. A Scheme for the Scottish Iron Age. In *The Iron Age in Northern Britain*, ed. A. L. F. Rivet. Edinburgh: Edinburgh University Press, pp. 1-15.

Plass, P. 1995. *The Game of Death in Ancient Rome: Arena Sport and Political Suicide*. Wisconsin: University of Wisconsin Press.

Price, N. 2014. Belief and Ritual. In *Vikings: Life and Legend*, eds. G. Williams, P. Pentz, and M. Wemhoff. London: British Museum Publications, pp. 162-195.

Raveri, M. 2002. Introduction. In *Japan at Play: the Ludic and the Logic of Power* eds J. Hendry and M. Raveri. London: Routledge, pp. 1-21.

REC Consultants 2016. *A Study of the Orkney Tourism Industry. Final Report to Orkney Islands Council*. Internal report by Reference Economic Consultants, dated June 2016.

Reed, A. 2007. Smuk is King. The Action of Cigarettes in a Papua New Guinea Prison. In *Thinking Through Things: Theorising Artefacts Ethnographically*, eds. Henare, M. Holbraad and S. Wastell. London: Routledge, pp. 32-46.

Renfrew, C. 2003. *Figuring it out*. London: Thames and Hudson.

Renfrew, C. 2004. Towards a Theory of Material Engagement. In *Rethinking Materiality*, eds. E. Demarrais, C. Gosden, and C. Renfrew. Cambridge: McDonald Institute, pp. 23-32.

Riches, D. 1975. Cash Credit and Gambling in a Modern Eskimo Economy. *Man* 10: 21-36.

Ritchie, A. 1977. Excavation of Pictish and Viking-age Farmsteads at Buckquoy, Orkney. Proceedings of the Society of Antiquaries of Scotland 108: 174-227.

Ritchie, G. and A. Ritchie 1991. *Scotland: Archaeology and Early Prehistory*. Edinburgh: Edinburgh University Press.

Ritchie, A. 2003. Paganism Among the Picts and the Conversion of Orkney. In *Sea Change: Orkney and Northern Europe in the Later Iron Age AD300-800*, eds. J. Downes and A. Ritchie. Brechin: Pinkfoot Press, pp. 3-10.

Ritchie, A. 2008. Gaming Boards. In *Inchmarnock: An early historic island monastery and its archaeological landscape, ed. C. Lowe*. Edinburgh: Society of Antiquaries of Scotland Monograph, pp. 116-128.

Robb, J. 2004. The Extended Artefact and the Monumental Economy: a Methodology for Material Agency. In *Rethinking Materiality: the engagement of mind with the material world*, eds. E. DeMarrais, C. Gosden and C. Renfrew. Cambridge: McDonald Institute Monograph, pp. 131-140.

Rubin, D. 1988. Go for the Skill. In *Remembering Reconsidered: Ecological and Traditional Approaches to the Study of Memory*, eds. U. Neisser and E. Winograd. Cambridge: Cambridge University Press, pp. 374-382.

St. Clair, A. 2003. *Carving as Craft: Palatine East and the Greco-Roman Bone and Ivory Carving Tradition*. Baltimore: Johns Hopkins University Press.

Sansi, R. 2015. *Art, Anthropology and the Gift*. London: Bloomsbury.

Schadler, U. 2007 The Doctor's Game - New Light on the History of Ancient Board Games. In *Stanway: An Elite Burial Site at Camulodunum'* eds. P. Crummy, S. Benfield, N. Crummy, V. Rigby, and D. Shimmin. London: Britannia Monograph Series No.24. Published by the Society for the Promotion of Roman Studies, pp. 359-375.

Schechner, R. 2002 [1994]. Ritual and Performance. In *Companion Encyclopedia of Anthropology,* ed. T. Ingold. London: Routledge, pp. 613-647.

Scott, L. 1948. Gallo-British colonies. The Aisled-roundhouse Culture in the North. *Proceedings of the Prehistoric Society* XIV: 46-125.

Scott, I. G. and A. Ritchie 2009. *Pictish and Viking-Age Carvings from Shetland*. Edinburgh: Royal Commission on the Ancient and Historical Monuments of Scotland.

Service, E. 1962. *Primitive Social Organisation*. London: Random House.

Service, E. 1975. *Origins of the State and Civilization*. London: W. W. Norton & Company.

Sharman, P. 2000. Steatite and Other Fine Stone Objects. In *Prehistoric Houses at Sumburgh in Shetland*, eds. J. Downes and R. Lamb. Oxford: Oxbow books.

Sharples, N. 1998. *Scalloway: A Broch, Late Iron Age Settlement and Medieval Cemetery in Shetland*. Oxford: Oxbow Monograph 82.

Sharples, N. 2003. From Monuments to Artefacts: Changing Social Relationships in the Later Iron Age. In *Sea Change: Orkney and Northern Europe in the Later Iron Age AD300-800* eds. J. Downes and A. Ritchie. Brechin: Pinkfoot Press, pp. 151-168.

Sharples, N. 2012. *A Late Iron Age Farmstead in the Outer Hebrides. Excavations at Mound 1, Bornais, South Uist*. Oxford: Oxbow Books.

Sheets-Johnstone, M. 2011. *The Primacy of Movement*. Amsterdam: John Benjamins Publishing.

Sjovold, T. 1962. *The Iron Age Settlement of Arctic Norway*. Tromsø: Tromsø Museums, Vol 1.

Sjovold, T. 1974. *The Iron Age Settlement of Arctic Norway*. Tromsø: Tromsø Museums, Vol 2.

Smith, A. 2007. Signs, Symbols and Games. In *Investigations in Sanday Orkney: Vol 1, Excavations at Pool, Sanday*, ed. J. Hunter. Kirkwall: Orcadian publications, pp. 507-514.

Spariosu, M. 1989. *Dionysus Reborn*. Ithica: Cornell University Press.

Stead, I. 1967. A La Tene III Burial at Welwyn Garden City. *Archaeologia* 101: 1-62.

Sutton-Smith, B. 1997. *The Ambiguity of Play*. Harvard: Harvard University Press.

Thomas, J. 2004. *Archaeology and Modernity*. London: Routledge.

Thorsteinsson, A. 1968. The Viking burial place at Pierowall, Westray, Orkney. In *The Fifth Viking Congress, Torshavn, July 1965* ed. B. Niclasen. Norwich, VT: Sutton Books, pp. 150-173.

Toner, J. P. 1995. *Leisure and Ancient Rome*. Cambridge: Polity Press.

Trail, J. 1890. Notes on the Further Excavations of Howmae, 1889. *Proceedings of the Society of Antiquaries of Scotland* 24: 451-461.

Turner, V. 1969. *The Ritual Process*. Venice: Aldine Press.

Turner, V. 1982. *From Ritual to Theatre*. New York: PAJ Publications

Turner, V. 1983. Liminal to Liminoid, in Play, Flow, and Ritual: An Essay in Comparative Symbology. In *Play Games and Sports in Cultural Contexts,* eds. J. C. Harris and R. J. Park. Illinois: Human Kinetics Books, pp. 123-164.

Turner, V. E. 1998. Ancient Shetland. London: Batsford.

Turner, V. E., A-C. Larsen, and O. A. Owen 2013. The Stone Settings of Balta. In *Viking Unst: Excavation and Survey in Northern Shetland 2006-2010,* eds. V. E. Turner, J. M. Bond, and A-C. Larsen. Lerwick: Shetland Amenity Trust, pp. 91-100.

Ucko, P. J. 1969. Ethnography and Archaeological Interpretation of Funerary Remains. *World Archaeology* 1 (2): 262-280.

Van Bremen, J. 2002. Japan in the World of Johan Huizinga. In *Japan at Play: the ludic and logic of power,* eds. J. Hendry and M. Raveri. London: Routledge, pp. 214-227.

Vygotsky, L. S. 1978. *Mind in Society: The Development of Higher Psychological Processes.* Harvard: Harvard University Press.

Watts, L. 2012. OrkneyLab: An Archipelago Experiment in Futures. In *Imagining Landscapes, Past, Present and Future,* eds. M. Janowski and T. Ingold. Farnham: Ashgate Press, pp 59-76.

Weiner, A. B. 1988. *The Trobrianders of Papua New Guinea*. New York: Holt, Rinehart and Winston Inc.

Whitehead, A. N. 1929. *Process and Reality: An Essay in Cosmology*. Cambridge: Cambridge University Press.

Whitehouse, H. 1996. Jungles and Computers: Neuronal Group Selection and the Epidemiology of Representations. *Journal of the Royal Anthropological Institute* (N.S.) 2: 99-116.

Whittington, E. M. 2001. *The Sport of Life and Death: the Mesoamerican Ball Game*. London: Thames and Hudson.

Woodburn, J. 1970. *Hunters and Gatherers: the Material Culture of the Nomadic Hadza*. London: British Museum Publications.

Woolf, A. 2007. *From Pictland to Alba 789-1070. The New Edinburgh History of Scotland*. Edinburgh: Edinburgh University Press.

Wynn, T. 1994. Tools and Tool Behaviour. In *Companion Encyclopedia of Anthropology*, ed. T. Ingold. London: Routledge, pp. 133-161.

Yalom, M. 2001. *Birth of the Chess Queen: A History*. New York: Harper Perennial.

Young, A. 1956. Excavations at Dun Cuier, Isle of Barra, Outer Hebrides. *Proceedings of the Society of Antiquaries of Scotland* 89: 290-328.

Youngs, S. M. 1983. The Gaming Pieces. In *The Sutton Hoo Ship Burial,* eds. C. Evans and R. Bruce-Mitford. London: British Museum Publications, Vol 3, pp. 853-874.